SPAIN

THE EXPAT SURVIVAL GUIDE

NativeSpain.™com

SPAIN

THE EXPAT SURVIVAL GUIDE

Yolanda Solo

NativeSpain.™com

First Published in Great Britain 2008 by www.BookShaker.com

Cover photograph © Sarah Jane Hartney. www.artwx.net

Typeset in Trebuchet

DISCLAIMER

To my husband Abelardo who had the courage to come to Spain and my children Brandon and Kira, who even in the darkest times manage to make me smile each and every day.

Praise for this book

Yolanda Solo's Spain Survival Manual is exactly what you need if you are thinking of moving to Spain. Even if you have already moved, you still need this comprehensive manual. There will be a lot happening that you never expected, and her manual will explain and simplify what is often a bewildering confusion of events.

Moving to Spain with rose-tinted glasses is one huge disappointment. Life gets in the way for one thing. Yolanda has a knack of highlighting the very things that will confuse, irritate, annoy or madden you. She explains in plain English why it is so, and why you have to adapt, change and accept them if you are serious about living in your new adopted country. As someone who had been living in Spain for a number of months when I purchased her book, I found myself constantly nodding in agreement at her insightful assessment of life in Spain as I read through the pages.

All the positive things about Spain that probably prompted you to consider moving there in the first place, are really only best enjoyed once all the bureacracy has been seen to. It's not easy, and there's no point in pretending it is. But Yolanda's book WILL make it a lot easier, and will shorten the time it takes to start fully enjoying your new life in Spain.

John Coutts

Contents

FOREWORD I
PREFACE III
INTRODUCTION V
HOW TO USE THIS BOOK VIII

CULTURE SHOCK...1
   MAÑANA, MAÑANA 1
   TIMETABLE 2
   HOLIDAYS 6
   NOISE 7
   ATTITUDE 9
   RELATIONSHIPS 10
BUREAUCRACY 15
   DOCUMENTATION 15
   NOTARY 17
   LACK OF CO-ORDINATION 18
   NIE & RESIDENTS CARD 20
EMPLOYMENT 23
   LOWER WAGES.. 25
   WORKING HOURS 26
   BLACK MARKET 26
   SELF-EMPLOYMENT 27
   AUTONOMO.. 28
   FREELANCE 29
   SETTING UP A COMPANY 30
FINANCE 33
   BANK CHARGES 33
   TAXES 34
   PESETAS 34
   DECIMAL.. 35
PROPERTY 37
   DOCUMENTS 37
   'B' MONEY 38
   ROOM WITH A VIEW 39

BEACH PROPERTIES 40
OFF-PLAN 40
RENOVATION PROJECTS 44
BUY-TO-LET 45
FINCAS 52

FAIL-PROOFING YOUR DREAMS 57
THE MOST COMMON REASONS FOR EXPAT FAILURE 57
SUCCESSFUL EXPATS 58
TESTING THE WATER 59

SUCCESS STORIES 65
RETURN TO ENGLAND? NOT LIKELY! 65
YOU'D HAVE TO BE MAD TO WANT TO LEAVE HERE 69
ALL WORTHWHILE IN THE END 73
GOING NATIVE IN MURCIA 75
MORATALLA HERE WE COME! 82

PLANNING & PREPARATION 87
LANGUAGE 87
FINANCE 92
WAGES 94
MORTGAGES 95
PROPERTY 97
SCHOOLS 98
HEALTH 101
CHANGE OF ADDRESS 103
FOREIGN EXCHANGE 104

CONCLUSION 107
RESOURCES 110
EMERGENCY NUMBERS 111
NON-EMERGENCY NUMBERS 111
ACCOUNTANTS 111
CURRENCY EXCHANGE 111
DOCUMENTS 112
DIRECTORIES 112
DRIVING 112
EMPLOYMENT 113
EXPAT RESOURCES 114
HEALTH 115

Holidays 115
Internet Providers 115
Government.. 115
Language 116
Online Translators 117
Lawyers 117
Maps... 118
Mobile Phones 118
Mortgages 118
Cajas de Ahorros (Building Societies) 119
Banks 120
News 121
Payments.. 122
Property 122
Radio 123
GLOSSARY... 124
TEMPLATES & CHECKLISTS 129
Relocation Budget 129
Change of Address Checklist 130
Renovation Budget... 131
Property Budget 132
ABOUT YOLANDA SOLO 135

Foreword

Hands up anyone who does not love Spain. Long, lazy, sunny days. Sangrias at sunset. Tapas at the local bar. Sounds like a dream. Maybe that's the problem...

Like moths to a flame, more and more expats are moving to Spain. In fact, official figures estimate that more than 1 in 10 residents in Spain are actually foreigners. People move to Spain because it is a wonderful place and it's seen as a land of opportunity. Many arrive from poorer countries, to establish a better life. Many retirees come from richer countries in what has affectionately been termed the "silver flight" to sunnier climates. Many others are the dreamers who see Spain as an escape from the traffic and rat race of home – a place to find more enjoyable work or to set up a more laid-back, lifestyle-business abroad.

Unfortunately the reality of life in Spain does not always match the postcard and many expatriates struggle in their newly-adopted Spanish home. This is where 'Spain: the expat survival guide' can help. Yolanda's generous sharing of her experiences makes for essential reading before you sell your 'home sweet home' and could help you avoid making the same mistakes that other expats make when moving to Spain.

Arriving from the UK, even Yolanda, with her good grasp of Spanish, had a steep learning curve. Spanish bureaucracy, culture shock, settling her children into a local school, family adjustments, buying property, working as an expat, nearly getting her car seized ... you name it and Yolanda's probably been through it. This makes her book a priceless source of hard-won information, tips, resources and advice for expats moving to Spain.

So whether you are bursting with excitement in anticipation of your move, or perhaps still a little indecisive, I highly recommend that you take the time to get Spain-savvy and read this book. As Yolanda says, *"The good news is that with the right attitude, proper planning and realistic expectations, moving to Spain may well be the best thing you have ever done."*

Go for it! Buena suerte y deseos Buenos!

Andrea Martins
www.expatwomen.com

Andrea Martins is the co-founder of ExpatWomen.com – a website designed to help all expatriate women, of all nationalities, living outside of their home country. Andrea and her business partner, Jill Lengré, set up their global website whilst living in the very similar Spanish-speaking environment of Mexico City, Mexico.

Preface

While there is a massive influx of foreigners relocating to or investing in Spain each year, there are also thousands leaving Spain – giving up on their dream, poorer, disillusioned and defeated.

Spain still continues to rank as the most popular expat destination with hundreds of thousands living in Spain or owning property there. The sunshine, the lifestyle, it's got to be better than where you are right now - hasn't it? Not necessarily. Thousands of expats have found out the hard way that moving to Spain, or buying a property there, can become a financial headache filled with struggle and heartache.

There are ways to avoid the problems that most expats are faced with, but which are impossible to know about beforehand. Hindsight is wonderful.

Most books on Spain talk about where to go, what to see and where to stay. They also talk about how fantastic the culture, the food and the lifestyle is. What they don't tell you is the price you have to pay for leaving your comfort zone - what you know and are familiar with.

"Culture Shock" is not just a short-term condition, some people never recover and find themselves giving it all up to go back home.

This book has been written to highlight some of the most important topics related to moving to or relocating to Spain, outlining the "hidden problems" faced by most expats.

- Learn how to avoid the mistakes most expats make
- Find out the crucial elements to making your experience a successful one
- Use the planning and preparation guides to make your experience as painless as possible!

Armed with this guide you can make your transition to Spanish life much easier and enjoy all the benefits this wonderful country has to offer much sooner.

I wish you every success!

Yolanda Solo
www.inlaluz.com

Introduction

Moving to or buying a property in a different country is very similar to getting married or having a baby. You plan, research, prepare and embark on your new venture feeling proud of having done everything in your power to make the transition as smooth and painless as possible. What you can't possibly do is realise the adjustments, sense of overwhelm and frustration that come with all of the above. And when you come face to face with the reality of the situation it is often accompanied by phrases such as OH MY GOD and LIFE WAS SO MUCH EASIER WHEN...

The key is in the invisible print, impossible to know beforehand and equally as impossible to fully grasp... the emotional consequences, the re-adjustments, changes of attitude and more.

The reasons for moving to Spain are many and varied, as are the reasons for buying a holiday home. Spain has long been a popular holiday destination with its convenient location within Europe and cheap airfares, particularly with the advent of low cost airlines. When compared to the relative doom and gloom of countries such as England with its bad weather, rat-race lifestyle, loss of community feeling it's easy to understand why so many people have considered moving to or have already moved to Spain.

Ironically, it is often the very things that make Spain such a great place to live that make you want to run screaming back to the relative normality of where you came from. The relaxed attitude, lack of urgency and the endless fiestas are fantastic once you become one of the natives, but they are also the very things that drive you to the brink of insanity when you are first entering the no-mans land of the newly arrived expat.

The biggest problem lies in the assumptions we make, not substantiated by anything other than our previous experiences in a different country, with a different culture. If I had a euro for every time I said, or heard other expats say (or rant) - "Surely they must have...?", "How they can they not...?", "How can they run a business like that...?" - I would be very rich indeed.

If you expect everything to work in the same way as it did at home, you will be severely disappointed! You have to accept that you are in a different country, with different methods. If you set your expectations to what you are used to, you will increase your frustration.

Be prepared for things to move more slowly and realise that you are not going to change the culture and you must either adapt or go crazy.

This book is not meant as a tourist guide of where to visit, how to get there etc. There is a wealth of information available on those subjects as well as the mechanics of buying a property. What is missing, is the vital information of the day to day realities of living in Spain and dealing with the Spanish way of life. If you remove those rose tinted spectacles, you will be better prepared and the transition to resident expat or property owner will be a much smoother path!

It is also important to note that while this book is based on real-life experiences, Spain is a vast country with marked regional differences. Not all expats will experience the same problems or face the same situations.

Spain is a beautiful country, with great people. But please, take my advice and ASSUME NOTHING!

IMPORTANT

Whilst all of the information in this guide was as accurate as possible at the time of first publication things do change. Please check for major updates at... *www.nativespain.com*

How to use this Book

 The star icon is a useful tip or reminder relating to the topic on the page.

 The globe icon indicates a useful website link. All of the resources are also listed at the end of the book as a quick reference guide. If any of the websites do not have an English translation simply go to *wordchamp.com* or use a translator such as *Google.com/language_tools*

 The tick icon indicates a checklist of things that are important to consider. You will find several blank checklists at the end of the book which you can print out and use to track your budget.

 The speech icon will show the meaning of any Spanish words.

 The looking-glass icon indicates a useful book or ebook - further details are available at the relevant website.

Culture Shock

MAÑANA, MAÑANA

As I said before, the very things that are great about Spain are the very things that drove my blood pressure through the roof.

The openness and friendliness of the Spanish was such a refreshing change from the cold, faceless, robotic lifestyle of London. It is great to have people look you in the eye, take an interest in you and make you feel like a human being. This does not apply however, when you are waiting in a queue of 20 people at the bank while the only cashier spends 15 minutes talking to a regular customer about how their operation went, what they had for dinner last night and how the niece's boyfriend's cousin's uncle's wife got a new "hair do" yesterday.

There is a distinct lack of urgency which can only be described as infuriating (to put it mildly). You've heard about it, you've laughed about

✪ Learn to breathe deeply!

✪ Only schedule one major administrative task a day

"We had to move three times while waiting for our house completion. The agents and lawyers kept telling us it would be done within two weeks because it was what we wanted to hear. Even when I thought I was being realistic giving it an extra five weeks, it wasn't enough!"

✪ Phone ahead to check opening hours to save wasted journeys

✪ Allow extra time for deadlines

"We were due to meet a potentially very important future business partner at 10am – an hour's drive away. At 9.40am my colleagues were still sitting having their breakfast with me jumping up and down telling them we had to leave NOW. To which they laughed and said – don't worry its Andaluz style to be late!"

it when you were just on holiday, but now you have to live with it. It won't seem like a funny little Spanish quirk when you have to deal with it day in, day out.

Emergencies aside, "time" is just not an issue. And this can apply to deliveries (which strangely seem to get delayed until after lunchtime if it gets too close to 2pm), appointments and meeting friends. Time is a very loose concept and if you arrange to meet a Spaniard at a certain time, it is not unusual for them to turn up late.

Whether its deliveries, appointments, documentation or anything else you are waiting for ALWAYS allow extra time and NEVER leave it until the last minute.

TIMETABLE

If you come from a 9-5 environment, or a large town/city with almost non-stop shop opening hours, you may find yourself wondering how the Spanish ever manage to get anything done. Between holidays, siestas and strange timetables you will most likely find yourself taking many wasted journeys and cursing – a lot.

While times may vary, as a general rule shops and offices open at 10am and stop at 2pm for siesta until 4 or 5pm when they open again until 8 or 9pm. Unless it is a government office which might only open until 3pm. Or unless it is one of the many fiesta days. Or unless there is a local holiday. Or unless they are working an intensive day during the summer. Or unless... Well you get the point, there are any number of variables.

Be aware that "full-time" can mean a workday of 10am to 2pm then 4pm until 8pm or 8.30am to 2pm then 4pm to 8pm and finishing early on a Friday

The moral of the story is not to assume a standard "work day" and not to try and schedule too many tasks in one day or you will only be setting yourself up for stress and frustration. A good rule of thumb is to schedule one main task a day i.e. getting your NIE number or going to the social security office.

It is always worth asking your employer if you can do a "jornada intensive" i.e. not take the long lunch break.

Oh and of course then there is "breakfast time". In many places there is the sacred coffee break in the mornings, generally at 10am, when you may see cafe bars filled with workmen, bank workers and the like.

Entertaining visitors? Well tourist areas aside, don't get to the restaurants too early. The Spanish eat much later and many restaurants don't even open until 9pm!

"I once arranged to meet a friend for breakfast at 9.10am. He said it had him chuckling for days because only an English person would be so precise. A Spaniard would say either 9 or 9.30 and probably not turn up until 10."

And finally, when you make an appointment or arrange to see someone, double check what TIME they mean. Midday to us may mean 12 o'clock, but to the Spanish midday is closer to 2pm as that is when they eat their lunch. So that could be two hours wasted waiting for someone!

The Spanish timetable is also something that you should take into consideration when looking for work.

There is still a tradition to go home for lunch between 2-4pm and return in the afternoon. This can create problems if you are the primary child carer in the family and also should you choose to find a job that is not close to where you live.

It can become a very long day if you hang around during the lunch period (which can be as long as three hours), or you could spend half the time travelling to and from your house.

If you work in catering then be prepared for long hours, particularly during the summer season, as the Spanish tend to go out much later and therefore stay out later. During the peak tourist season bars will stay open until the last customer leaves – and this may not be until five in the morning – or later!

Teaching English is another favourite for many expats. However, if you are giving private classes or even teaching in an academy, you may find yourself working until 10pm at night. The Spanish finish work later, so will expect to have classes later.

"It was really difficult to find a well-paid job to fit around the school hours. And the best paid jobs meant I had to do split shifts which didn't finish until 8pm. By the time I arrived home, it was almost time for the children to go to bed."

HOLIDAYS

You also need to know that there is not one standard set of holidays for the whole of Spain. There are local holidays, as well as regional and national holidays. And when the holidays fall near a weekend the Spanish may do what they call a "*puente*" (bridge) so although the holiday might only be one day, certain businesses, offices and schools might take an extra day. For example, let's say the holiday is on a Thursday, for many people the Friday will also be included as holiday.

And depending where you are in Spain, you could well find that during the hottest month of August it is impossible to get anything finalised. A lot of companies will close completely or have only a skeleton staff. This is because many people take the whole of the month off. Not a great time to be buying a house for example!

And then in December there is a national holiday on the 6th and the

⊗ Get a list of national, regional and local holidays

⊕ Holidays in Spain

info.mtas.es/infpuntual/Fiest as2007/calendariolab_02.htm

⊗ Always over-estimate the time it takes to get things done

8th so there could be a "Puente" on the 7th. Well, why go in to work for just one day? And then there is Christmas (although they don't have Boxing Day holiday) and New Year … and you breathe a sigh of relief as you think things have returned to normality. But no, there is yet another holiday on the 6th January for *Reyes* (Three Kings).

NOISE

There is a distinct difference in the noise levels in Spain, which will affect you in all sorts of ways.

To many people, the Spanish simply seem to shout a lot of the time. They are outgoing, lively and expressive which means that they can have a heated debate over the smallest issue. To the untrained eye these "debates" actually look more like arguments (the whole hand waving while talking also adds to the drama) when in fact they are just having a bit of friendly banter.

It's all in the timing…

"We arrived in December thinking we'd have a great time as Spain is a 'party town'. On Christmas Eve NOTHING was open, even the bars shut at 9pm. And a similar thing happened on New Year's Eve. The Spanish just laughed at me saying that Christmas Eve is family night and they go out after 1am and on New Year's Eve things don't get going until 2 or 3 in the morning."

"I live in a finca so thought I would be away from it all. But they had a fiesta in the town nearby and I was woken up by a concert starting at 3.30am! I was outraged which my neighbours thought was hysterical, as to them it was perfectly normal."

The Spanish have a much higher tolerance for noise of all sorts including but not limited to: screaming kids that appear to run riot, dogs barking all night, tooting car horns and general debate which can be heard a mile away.

If you choose to live in a Spanish apartment block or a townhouse, while you are planning to go to bed at around 11pm, many Spanish will just be getting ready to go out! Even worse, in the heat of the summer, the evening is the very time they tend to come out and you could find your neighbours in the streets enjoying the cool night air until 2 or 3 am.

So if you think that a little flat in the village square is quaint, think that it will also be the central hive of activity for the locals until the early hours, especially if it has cafes or bars.

ATTITUDE

Do not expect please and thank you for every transaction. It is used much less frequently than for example the English would use it and can take some getting used to. "Give me a..." can sound very abrupt without the customary "Could you please..." or "Can I have..." before it.

This is just one of the reasons that the Spanish can appear to be really rude to those from "quieter" cultures. They are generally more direct, more open, more "forceful" and much noisier!

And you won't find a Spanish person sitting waiting like a lemon for half an hour if someone can't be bothered to serve them. While the foreigners stand patiently and obediently waiting to be served, be it in a shop or bar, all around them the Spanish are getting served left, right and centre because they are the first ones to speak up when an

 Raise your tone of voice a little and you are likely to get served much faster.

"I had to laugh. A friend of mine had been waiting for a beer for about 30 minutes and was getting more irate by the minute as all around her the Spanish were getting served first. I told her she had to be more bolshy and pushed my way to the bar next to her, raised my tone of voice and got served almost straight away."

Get some attitude!

assistant says "who's next?" If you're not fast... you're last.

"My mother went to Spain to see her family after a long absence of 8 years. Leaving the arrivals lounge she was overjoyed to see them again and after a touching hug and kiss their first words to her were 'my God you're fat'."

Another side effect of the Spanish being so open is that they tend to stare... directly and without shame. No sideways glances, no sneak peeks, just blatant staring. You may well spend the first few months wondering if you are walking around exposing yourself, or if you have left the house wearing your pyjamas.

Then there is the *"Oiga"* (which sounds like the equivalent of "Oy you" but literally means "listen") to attract your attention as well as the "pssssst" hissing sound used for the same affect.

RELATIONSHIPS

Moving to Spain is not like going on a second honeymoon. If you and your partner are having problems at home, these will become magnified in Spain. Some sources state that the divorce rate amongst expats is 40% higher than those who have not relocated.

You won't have your friends, family or work mates around to distract you from all the little things that drive you crazy. Your partner may well be your one and only source of entertainment for a considerable length of time before you start work/business, make friends etc.

It can take many months to build up even a small group of friends and your choice will be limited to the expats in the area if you do not speak Spanish.

Additionally, the dynamics of a relationship often change when you move abroad. Perhaps the main breadwinner suddenly has to stay at home while the partner goes out to work. Or the inability to get the equivalent job they had at home and have to resort to more "menial work" can cause resentment and discontent. All of this will affect your relationship, particularly in the most stressful first 12 months.

While of course it is a generalisation, it seems that women suffer more with missing family and friends,

"My husband had to become the 'housewife' when we moved to Spain. He didn't speak Spanish and I had come over with work. One classic comment he came out with was that he felt like a slave just cooking and cleaning!"

⚝ If one partner is relocating for work, ensure the other partner has a job, hobby or circle of friends to avoid feeling isolated.

11

while men tend to suffer more frustration learning the language and adjusting to the change in work opportunities.

⊛ Learn Spanish before you arrive to help you integrate as soon as possible in local life.

And what if one partner is happy with the move and the other is not? Perhaps one of you loves Spain from the moment you land, while the other just can't wait to leave? Many couples are faced with the choice of returning home when one partner is unhappy... or going their separate ways (which happens much more often than you might imagine.)

⊛ Find a way to keep regular contact with those at home to avoid feeling isolated e.g. phone, email, messenger

One of many examples is a middle-aged couple that move to Spain. The husband immediately gets to know the locals and expats in the area and starts doing odd-jobs to make a living. The wife however, is not so outgoing and finds it harder to mix with strangers. In addition, she may be used to having friends and family close by to visit and support her.

⊛ Include holidays to visit friends and family in your budget

Result? He loves it whilst she is bored, isolated and desperately misses the close circle of friends and family she had at home.

If either one of you has any doubts, do not put your eggs in one basket and sell your house at home, pack your bags and head off into the sunshine hoping for the best. Sun, sea and sangria does not cure all ills.

✪ If financially possible, do not sell your home until you are sure both partners are happy with the move

Bureaucracy

DOCUMENTATION

Also not so affectionately known as bloody bureaucracy, there is a wealth of paperwork to wade through and the inefficiencies of the system make even the Spanish despair.

Again there are regional differences, and so I am told (by those from the north of Spain), the north tends to be more efficient and "formal" than the south of Spain. Nevertheless it would be very foolish to assume the mañana mañana attitude includes the debt recovery systems e.g. Hacienda (tax office) and Social Security. That is one area where in even the sleepiest parts of Spain they seem to have wholeheartedly embraced the age of computers to generate fines for late payment of taxes or filing of tax returns etc.

It is important to get local advice whenever possible. You should contact a lawyer, accountant etc.

"I thought I would save money and do everything myself. Instead I've paid over €600 in fines and nearly had my car seized for not paying €72 to social security."

✪ Include the services of professionals in your budget – at least for the first year.

✪ Get a NIE number

✪ Keep copies of EVERYTHING

✪ Get all payments officially stamped

✪ Phone ahead to check opening times and location of offices

✪ Always chase up paperwork – don't wait for people to get back to you just because they said they would.

"You couldn't make it up... A tax return was rejected and the submitter fined because the return was 1 CENT out. He couldn't do a bank transfer nor write a cheque for such a small amount and the tax office did not accept payments directly!"

✸ Set up direct debits for as many payments as possible

✸ Question EVERYTHING

✸ Get everything in writing

✸ Ask a Spanish speaking friend, colleague or representative to check all important documents

that works within your province. Why? In Huelva for example car tax is paid between July and September, yet in Badajoz – the province right next door – the taxes are paid from January!

While you can organise all the necessary paperwork yourself, I strongly recommend that you include the services of a local gestoria (administrative office), accountant or lawyer who can deal with the Spanish administration on your behalf. Otherwise you will be navigating the bureaucratic maze of a new country with new rules, procedures, deadlines and penalties, all of which you are unfamiliar with.

While it may seem like an extravagance, based on the experience of expats, the time you will save on navigating the minefield of Spanish bureaucracy and the money you will save on fines for not filing form x, y or z will more than compensate for the expense.

It is of course possible to complete the necessary basic steps yourself.

However, dedicate the appropriate amount of time to it. Do not rely solely on a book or website for information – use them merely as a guide not a bible - unless they are written by professionals working in the relevant fields. Information and requirements change all the time and it would be impossible to keep up to date with legislation unless you are a practising professional.

NOTARY

The notary (*notaria*) is a perfect example of what appears to be an unnecessary, time-wasting and expensive step in the bureaucratic process. A "middleman", the notary's function is supposed to be to ensure there are no irregularities when setting up things like mortgages, car leases etc.

For example:
- End of year tax returns must be rubber stamped by the notary so he can "confirm" that the signatures on the return are genuine and belong to the company directors. Even though you can just sign

- Social Security
  www.seg-social.es
- Tax Office
  www.aeat.es
- Vehicle Licensing
  www.dgt.es
- Ministry of Science & Education
  www.mec.es
- Ministry of Work & Social Affairs
  www.mtas.es
- Ministry of the Interior
  www.mir.es
- Treasury
  www.meh.es
- Ministry for Public Administration
  www.map.es
- Electronic DNI
  www.dnielectronico.es
- Ministry of Public Works -
  www.fomento.es
- Ministry of Foreign Affairs
  www.mae.es
- Housing Ministry
  www.mviv.es

"When someone says 'don't worry, leave it with me…' begin to worry"

⊛ Delegate your administrative tasks to a gestoria, accountant or lawyer whenever your budget allows.

17

"I recently had a problem with being registered for Social Security as Autonomo and was trying to get de-registered. However, my accountant had done it online and the Seguridad Social would not accept the online submission as proof I had been deregistered in Hacienda.

"So I went to Hacienda only to be told that Seguridad Social should have asked them for the information direct as they had an agreement to share information between the two government bodies. They would not however give me a copy of the official date I was de-registered and would only give me another form confirming it.

CONTINUES...

the return and get your accountant to take it to the notary for you. And you get to pay for the privilege.

• I had a car lease for which I borrowed money from the bank. I paid the bank, they confirmed the debt was paid. Only 2 months later when I went to sell the car did I find out I had to go to the *Registro Mercantil* to remove the record of my "debt" before it could be transferred. For this I first had to go to the bank, get a form confirming I had paid the loan and on the way to the *Registro*, stop off at the notary so he could confirm that the stamp on the form from the bank was authentic!

LACK OF CO-ORDINATION

One of the reasons for suggesting the use of a local gestoria is the astounding lack of co-ordination between and within government offices, shops, services etc.

When you apply for something you may get sent away saying that it cannot be processed without a "vital" missing document. So off you trot, having wasted a morning, retrieve the missing document, trudge back to the office only to find that a different person serving you does not even ask for it, or worse, says you don't need it!

It is very important you get everything you are told confirmed, ideally in writing. Especially in relation to contracts, major purchases and taxes. You can easily misunderstand what you are told when you are new to the language and will have no recourse if it is your word against theirs.

It is equally possible that having gained a bit of confidence in the old lingo you negotiate in Spanish and away you go proud of yourself for how well you have done, only to discover for example that the tax office were not in fact offering you a rebate, but actually giving you a final reminder!

...CONTINUED

"Back again to Seguridad Social to be told it was ridiculous, no such agreement existed with Hacienda and that without the copy of the original form they would not de-register me. If I wrote a letter explaining the situation, attaching the notice of de-registration from Hacienda, they would CONSIDER it. Meanwhile I am being threatened with having my car seized by them for not making payments to a system they won't let me de-register from.

"Back to Hacienda, to fill out a form, which then has to be sent to Madrid and returned to me. So much for de-regulation."

- ◎ Gestoria - Administrative agents (not necessarily accountants or lawyers) that process documentation
- ◎ Hacienda - The tax agency in Spain
- ◎ Autonomo - Self Employed
- ◎ Seguridad Social - Social Security

- ⊕ Legal Advice
  www.iabogado.com

"The first time we did a major food shop after arriving was at Carrefour Hypermarket. Having spent an hour filling up two trolleys, queuing for another 15 minutes grumbling about the people in front taking so long, we passed everything through the till and bagged it all up. Having done such a big shop I didn't have enough cash so gave

CONTINUES...

NIE & RESIDENTS CARD

The NIE is the *Numero de Identification de Extranjeros* i.e. Foreigners Identification Number which is the equivalent of the DNI (*Documento Nacional de Identidad*) for the Spanish nationals.

If you search the internet for the rules on whether or not you need to have a residents card you will undoubtedly find 20 differing opinions. One will say you do not need it, another will say you do, yet another will give you a time scale. ALWAYS go to the source i.e. the relevant government website or ask your lawyer who should be up to date with current legislation.

For example at extranjeros.mtas.es you will find the latest information including all the rules for residency and working in Spain, which is now provided in English.

On their leaflet *"Regulations Governing EU citizens in Spain"* they state that:

"EU citizens are free to enter, leave, travel or live in Spain and may also... engage in any economic activity, either as paid employees or self-employed, service providers or students, under the same conditions as Spanish citizens."

However it also goes on to say that after three months in Spain you should register for a NIE number.

So while theoretically it is not necessary to get one if you are an EU citizen, as you have the right to live and work in other EU countries, you will be asked for ID for countless transactions including:

- Buying a house
- Buying a car
- Setting up utilities
- Car insurance
- Bank accounts
- When receiving registered post
- When paying by credit or debit card

Then there is the residents card (*Tarjeta de Residencia*) which again in theory you do not need, however

...CONTINUED

her my credit card and she said something about my identity card. When she saw the gormless look on my face she obviously realised I didn't have one and asked for my passport instead. Which obviously I didn't have either as I had only planned to go the supermarket, not get on a plane.

"Turns out however, you can't use a credit or debit card without showing some sort of photo ID to prove the card is yours. So no cash, no ID, no shopping! Just a very red faced foreigner hightailing it out of the supermarket."

⭐ If you plan to stay longer than three months get a NIE number

⭐ Ask an accountant about the advantages of getting a residents card

⭐ Always carry identification with you, as it is a legal requirement in Spain

you get tax advantages such as paying less tax on rental income, tax breaks on wealth tax and other benefits. But you then need to be careful about how this affects your situation in your home country to ensure you are not paying double taxation.

The only way to ensure you navigate the bureaucratic maze successfully is to get professional advice.

Employment

A staggering amount of people move to Spain with a limited amount of funds assuming that they will be able to find a job without having fluent Spanish.

It is essential that you have one of the following before moving to Spain:

- An offer of employment

or

- Enough "spare" cash to live for at least six months, preferably a year or more. This should not be money to buy a property, car or any other extras but in place of wages, should you not find a source of income.

Myth: I don't need to speak Spanish to find a job

Even if you move to areas with a high density of expats and English-speaking businesses you are going to be very limited in your choice of jobs. A large number of people will end up working in bars, cleaning rental properties, or working for a real estate company on commission only.

Job Search Websites
www.ambientjobs.com
www.empleo.net
www.exposure-eu.com
www.global-recruiter.com
www.faster.es
www.lnfoempleo.com
www.nfojobs.net
www.jobssbroad.com
www.jobtoasterspain.com
www.laborman.es
www.miltrabajos.com
www.monster.es
www.oficinaempleo.com
www.recruitspain.com
www.secretariaplus.com
www.talentsearchpeople.com
www.thinkspain.com
www.trabajar.com
www.trabajos.com
www.wemploy.com

Learn Spanish to improve your job prospects

ETTs (Temp agencies)
www.adecco.es
www.empresaslman.com
www.flexiplan.es
www.manpower.es
www.randstad.es
www.select.es
www.tutor-rrhh.com

Myth: I can set up a business catering to the "huge" expat market

While there are indeed a lot of expats in Spain, and high concentrations of them in some areas, they are just a tiny fraction of the whole population i.e. your potential customer base. And if you are catering to the tourist trade your business will only be seasonal. And don't forget you will still need to do all the paperwork, get supplies and deliveries etc. all of which will mean dealing with Spanish people... in Spanish.

Myth: I can live off the money from the sale of the house back home

Unless you have established investments - a pension or other regular income - a lump sum, however large it may seem, will only last for a limited amount of time. It also gives you a false sense of security giving you a great excuse delay creating a source of income in Spain (job, business, etc) until its too late and your money has all been spent.

LOWER WAGES

It is important to realise that wages are substantially lower in Spain, particularly for the unskilled jobs that most expats will be applying for.

When you are planning your finances do not base your budget on the level of wages from your home country. Research jobs you might consider in the area you are moving to whether through the internet, or local papers on one of your visits there.

☆ Research jobs and level of salaries before moving

While those moving to the large cities will have the advantage of a greater variety of job opportunities and most likely a higher rate of pay, the cost of living in cities such as Barcelona and Madrid is also much higher than other parts of Spain. Property and rental prices are very high so you could find yourself stuck in the cycle of living to work just to meet expenses.

☆ Expect to earn up to a third of your current income when you move to Spain

WORKING HOURS

As mentioned before, Spanish working hours will most likely be very different to those you are used to. Be sure to confirm if you are required to work a split-shift or the afternoon shift which may not start until 5pm.

BLACK MARKET

There are of course many people who work for cash in hand and do not claim any earnings. While this may provide a short-term solution, it is of course tax evasion with the corresponding heavy penalties if you get caught. Banks are obliged to report if large sums of cash are paid into accounts which it is rumoured can start from as little as €2000.

✪ Confirm what benefits you will be entitled to if your employer asks to pay you part cash, part declared earnings

✪ Make sure you have sufficient health, sickness and unemployment cover if you work cash in hand.

Or it may be employers who pay you cash in hand to avoid having to pay social security payments for employees. This is cheaper for them, but also means that you will have zero or limited social security cover should you be unable to work through sickness for example.

Also, if you ever plan to buy a house, get a loan for a car or any other form of credit, you will be asked for proof of earnings on which to base your loan. If you have no work history and no regular earnings going into your bank account, you will have no way of proving your ability to pay.

Consider the effects on your credit rating if you only work for cash.

SELF-EMPLOYMENT

Also known as the expat pipe dream. Go to a new country, start your own business! Consider that just those two things are in the top ten list of most stressful life events. Without even factoring in moving house (also in the top ten) and the language disadvantage.

Consider VERY carefully if you can afford to work for yourself

If you don't speak Spanish your potential market is massively reduced and will be greatly affected by the holiday seasons if you can only cater to the expat or tourist trade. In addition, you are likely to overestimate your income as the prices you charge will almost certainly have to be much lower than expected to compete.

Self-employment is an expensive minefield of paperwork for the uninitiated and should only be undertaken if you have a substantial amount of financial backing, be it savings, assets or investors.

⊗ Ask all of your service providers for special deals they offer to autonomos e.g. mobile phone operators, banks, etc

AUTONOMO

A self-employed person is called "Autonomo" and is required to pay a hefty social security premium of a minimum of approx. 235 euros per month, regardless of whether any income has been earnt. Not to mention accountant's fees, tax returns etc. and the mountain of bureaucratic hoops they must go through.

"I once got a fine of 150 euros for registering €0 income for the quarter just 3 days late."

For example:

Not only is the Autonomo social security system different to the general one, there are also two different social security systems for autonomos! If you work for yourself you will pay under one system and then should you decide to form a company you could also

⊕ AEAT - tax office online *www.aeat.es*

pay at the same time the social security autonomo charges for a company director.

Example on monthly earnings (these figures are for illustration purposes only):

Gross earnings €1000

15% IRPF (tax) retention €150

Min. Social Security quota €205

Accountant fee €80

Net Earnings €565

So if your monthly income is relatively low, you will be paying a huge chunk in tax, social security and administration!

FREELANCE

If you do intend to work for yourself but only have odd jobs every now and again, it is worthwhile becoming a freelance so you do not get crippled by social security and tax payments.

Freelance is suitable for those that have irregular work of perhaps only a few days a month, or projects at irregular intervals e.g. writers,

There is a separate Social Security "regime" for autonomos and you must make sure you de-register from it as well as at the Tax Office should you stop working for yourself.

Make sure you get all documents of registration (alta) and de-registration (baja) officially stamped.

Freelance co-operative for workers with ad hoc projects and irregular income...
www.freelance.es

If you are likely to need credit i.e. a mortgage, make sure you have a regular amount getting paid into your account.

Official Credit Institute - loans for small businesses operating in Spain... *www.ico.es*

CIF - *Codigo de Identificacion Fiscal* (Fiscal identification number)

graphic designers etc. So if you have a project that will last 2 weeks, you inform the Freelance company and they register you for social security for the two weeks you are working. You therefore only pay the two weeks of social security you are actually working – and earning – rather than the whole month.

They also process all of your invoices, retain a portion of your earnings for tax, submit your tax returns and generally take care of the administrative headaches for you.

SETTING UP A COMPANY

Setting up your own business is not for the faint hearted! An expensive and complicated affair in your own country, imagine the added problems you will face in Spain.

First are the costs involved which include approximately €1000 for the setting up of the company (notary, registry, CIF) and approximately €3000 which must be lodged in the company account. This can be withdrawn once the company is set up but is still a sizeable amount of cash you need to have available.

If you are going to the trouble of setting up a company rather than working as an autonomo or freelance, it is likely that you are going to be operating on a larger scale than a one-man band. Perhaps you will be opening an office or shop to offer services or products in which case you will also have to apply for the appropriate licences such as health and safety, building works or licencia de apertura.

Licencia de Apertura – Opening Licence for premises required to legally operate a business and sell goods to clients entering your premises.

Throw into the equation Spanish bureaucracy, mañana mañana syndrome on top of the language barrier and you can, without hesitation, add a year to the process of setting up your business.

Underestimate your income and overestimate your expenses

Consider this:

Use a professional to deal with as many of the bureaucratic procedures as you can afford

- **Year 1** - Period of adjustment, house-hunting, settling-in and deciding on which business you will set up.

- **Year 2** - Finding premises, setting up the company, applying for licences... waiting for licences, contractors, building works...

- **Year 3** – First fully operational year of the company – and few companies are a resounding success in the first year as it takes time to build up the business.

So while it is of course possible to do all of the above in a shorter period of time, it is important to factor in the possibility that it could well take this long before you begin to operate successfully – and earn a respectable amount of money!

Before undertaking any of the self-employment models – be it autonomo, freelance or setting up a company – calculate all of the associated costs involved (which are likely to underestimate) versus potential income (which you are likely to overestimate).

Finance

BANK CHARGES

In much of Europe it has been many years since bank charges were for anything other than loan interest or overdraft charges. In Spain however, you can find yourself paying hundreds of Euros a year in charges from the accumulation of some services including:

- Receiving money from abroad
- Money transfers within Spain
- Account maintenance
- Cash withdrawals from other banks etc.
- Mobile phone top ups

If you do not use a cashpoint from your own bank, the charge for withdrawing €500 can vary anywhere from €0.30 to €25 depending on which bank you choose. As well as some banks charging you for on-screen account balances.

✪ Read the small print when joining a bank and compare their bank charges

✪ Check how much they charge for receiving overseas payments

"I thought I was being clever paying off my car lease loan and saving myself 3 years of interest, until I paid off what I thought was the outstanding loan amount. My bank statement showed an extra 2600 euros had been taken out! The bimbo at the bank calmly told me it was the 16% IVA that was payable that she 'forgot' to tell me about."

European Commission - information on taxation agreements
www.ec.europa.eu/taxation_customs/taxation/index_en.htm

Always ask if the amount you are quoted includes IVA before signing anything.

"Where I live even the younger generation sometimes use pesetas. When I went to buy a car I calculated the equivalent price in euros as €9000 – the car dealer meant €11,000!"

If you decide to top up your pay-as-you-go card with €50, you will find you only get €43 on your phone... €7 goes to VAT!

TAXES

A standard rate of 16% IVA (VAT) is charged on most goods and services in Spain and is very often not included in the "sale price" of items such as cars, houses etc. which can leave you with an additional bill of several thousands euros.

Always assume there will be IVA (VAT) added to anything you buy or any service you use.

PESETAS

A surprising number of people still use pesetas, which can be really confusing. However as a general rule 1 million pesetas = 6000 euros for ease of calculation. You need to be aware of this when buying anything substantial such as a car or a house as a misunderstanding when converting from pesetas to euros could cost you several thousand euros.

Always confirm the equivalent amount in euros if someone gives you a price in pesetas.

Check with an exchange rate calculator

DECIMAL

Beware the decimal point. In Spain it is the opposite to the UK and they use the decimal point to separate thousands and a comma to separate the cents.

€2.000,00 = two thousand euros

So be careful when writing cheques and asking for bank transfers!

Currency Converter - although his is not the exchange rate you would get if changing money at the bank it is a good estimating tool when converting money – and it includes Pesetas! *www.oanda.com*

Property

If you are lucky, you will already have found and purchased the house you are going to live in before you make the move. Some, however, will face the potentially painful process of house-hunting after arrival.

DOCUMENTS

There are two property registries – *Catastro* (land registry) and *Registro de la Propriedad* (property registry).

If you are buying a property with a plot (as opposed to an urbanisation), your property will most likely be registered with both entities. However, the information held by each does not always match!

It is essential to confirm that any property you buy is free of any liens or encumbrances a.k.a. charges, or you will be liable to pay these. Charges will be against the property and not against the owners. Your lawyer should check this for you. Or you can request a "Nota Simple"

Questions to ask ... to name but a few

- Is the property legally registered?
- Is the land legally registered?
- Is the property free of charges
- Are the taxes on the property up-to-date?
- Is the property/plot included in any future re-development or urbanisation of the area?
- Are there community fees payable?

Property Registry - you can request a copy of a *nota simple* online... *www.registradores.org*

which is a summary of the property details and any charges against it.

◎ 'A' Money - declared funds

◎ 'B' Money - undeclared funds

'B' MONEY

B Money – is a percentage of the purchase price that many sellers will want paid separately to the purchase contract and often in cash. This is to reduce their capital gains liability as the lower the sale price on paper, the smaller amount of taxable profit they have made "on paper". If you have found your ideal property you may be tempted to accept this. However you should consider that if you pay a lower purchase price on paper, the greater will be the "paper profit" that you make when you come to sell your house and the greater will be your capital gains liability.

Although illegal (tax evasion) it is still a very widespread practice and many sellers will not sell the property without a large portion of 'B' money.

ROOM WITH A VIEW

If you buy a property in a rural area that is relatively close to the town, you should be prepared that in the not so distant future, the area surrounding you will be developed.

⊗ Don't count on that wonderful view being there forever!

Spain is a "relatively" new country with a lot of expansion still planned, particularly in areas not on the already popular costas.

In the same way, if you buy an apartment with a sea view that is not front line but has an empty plot in front of it, you can almost certainly guarantee that at some point another developer will build on it, possibly obstructing your view.

⊗ Be sure to check any future developments planned in the area

BEACH PROPERTIES

Imagine you find your dream property where you step out from your terrace directly on to the beach. Idyllic? Not if your property is subject to the Coastal Law.

Always use a lawyer

According to this relatively recent law, no property may be built within 200m of the beach. And worse, in some areas, where there are properties illegally built on the beach, there is talk of knocking them down within the next ten years. The owner will obviously not volunteer this information so USE A LAWYER.

OFF-PLAN

Off-Plan means that you are buying the property before it is completed and often before building has even begun. It can be a very attractive prospect as you only have to pay a percentage of the purchase price, with the balance due at completion - generally in 18 months to two year's

Always get payments confirmed by the bank and developer

time - or small stage payments throughout construction.

The claims made range from "purchase at 30% below value", "buy and sell before completion" and "make a huge profit". All of which are perfectly true... in theory.

Only buy what you can afford ... do not be seduced by the "potential" profit

Assuming the property is not overpriced

You are given the discount for buying off-plan and the price is expected to increase by the discount given by the time construction is finished.

Assuming you are allowed to sell before completion

Not all developers allow you to do this. Make sure that it is specifically written into the contract that you have the right to sell before completion. If not, you will have to assume the costs associated with completion such as mortgages, lawyer's fees, notary etc.

Make sure you do not miss any stage payments – or you may be in breach of contract

If you are buying in a large urbanisation where you are allowed to sell before completion, you will be competing with all the other buyers trying to do the same. In addition, it

If you want to sell before completion, ensure it is written into the contract.

41

is harder to sell an off-plan contract than a completed property. You should allow a minimum of six months to sell the property.

Get a copy of the contract in your language.

If you decide to keep the property, be prepared for delays. As a general rule developers are allowed a six month grace period to allow for delays during construction. In addition to that, once the property is completed, they must apply for a "licence of first occupation" before owners are allowed to move in. Without this licence, no utilities can be connected.

Factor in 6-12 months delay for off-plan projects.

It can happen that building is delayed by a year and more, so do not start planning your rental bookings according to the date given to you by the developer. Wait until you have the keys in your hand.

Do not plan rentals or moving dates until you have the keys in your hand!

For the same reason, if you are planning to live there permanently, do not base the sale of your house or moving date on the completion date given by the developer. Always have a backup plan. If you are renting in peak season expecting imminent completion, you may find it hard to extend the rental contract or find yourself paying extortionate rates if you have to move to another property.

And when at last you get to visit your property, the very first thing you should do is a snagging list. This is a list of all the things that are wrong with the property.

Ideally you should get a professional to do this as there are many things that an untrained eye might miss. The New Homes Bureau estimates that it should take 1-2 hours for a one bedroom flat!

This is, of course, yet another expense. However poor quality builds could cost you thousands in repairs over the years, which makes the services of a qualified engineer to do the snagging list cheap by comparison.

⊛ NEVER agree to make a snagging list until the property is completely finished and cleaned.

"A typical three-bedroom, two-bathroom house will have more than 650 different points to check in the building and its surroundings and InspectaHomeSpain analysis has found an average of 74 defects per property based on inspections carried out."

www.eyeonspain.com

⊕ Inspecta Homes Spain
inspectahomespain.com

⊘ DIY Guide To Snagging –
www.diysnagreport.com

43

RENOVATION PROJECTS

The cost of renovations can mount up substantially even if you think the building is structurally sound. It is worth doing some rough calculations of what you would plan to do to the house before you buy. Make sure to include expensive items such as replacing doors, windows, tiles, roof, terraces, swimming pool etc. If the house needs a lot of work, consider knocking it down and starting from scratch!

An old house will still be an old house made good if you renovate and you may find yourself continually repairing problems such as damp. If you build from scratch you will know how it is built and can ensure proper drainage, insulation etc.

Also, just because you have bought a large plot of land does not automatically entitle you to build whatever you want. Generally, you will only be able to build to the same dimensions of the original registered building. If there is no

⊛ Always get a lawyer to check if the property is registered and the extent of the building permissions applicable to the property.

⊛ The responsibility is yours to get the professionals to do the appropriate checks.

⊛ Visit the property more than once before buying to see past the bargain you think you are getting.

⊛ Make a note of everything you think you will eventually replace - it will most likely add up to more than a lick of paint.

⊛ Check the building regulations if you want to add an extension.

building on the land you are likely to only get permission to build a warehouse - if that.

In the past, owners ignored the regulations, built the house and waited four years until it became possible to register it, happy to pay the relatively small fine. However, legislation is being tightened and gone are the days where you could virtually guarantee getting approval. Instead, there is now talk of hefty fines and the tearing down of illegal buildings.

BUY-TO-LET

Buy-To-Let is also known as pay-for-itself-property for the uninitiated first timer. The theory is that you buy a property, furnish it and as if by magic it will pay for itself as the rental earnings will cover the mortgage.

It doesn't always work out that way. Estate agents may exaggerate the rental potential to get a sale; or rental agents may promise to get six months worth of bookings a year; or even you as the owner may use the property for

⊘ Renovation Budget

- ❏ Bathroom
- ❏ Doors
- ❏ Extensions
- ❏ Fencing
- ❏ Flooring
- ❏ Heating
- ❏ Kitchen
- ❏ Landscaping
- ❏ Re-wiring electrics
- ❏ Re-plastering
- ❏ Roof
- ❏ Swimming Pool
- ❏ Terrace
- ❏ Well
- ❏ Windows

If you need to address all of the above, seriously consider building from scratch!

friends and family in the peak season when you're most likely to get rental clients!

Regardless of what anyone may tell you, as the "investor" you must take the necessary steps to ensure that your buy-to-let is a success and not just a financial headache.

✪ Only buy what you can afford!

Myth: The rent will cover the mortgage

You will need time to furnish the property, landscape the garden, get rental clients, etc. All of which could easily take upto a year during which you will have to cover the mortgage payments.

✪ Do not assume you will rent out the property for six months of the year

A realistic estimate is you may be able to let out your property for 12 weeks of the year, which leaves a long 40 weeks with no income.

You should not consider a buy-to-let property if you are not able to pay the mortgage without any rental income – this is a bonus.

Myth: I'll buy cheap furniture because it will just get ruined

While it would be crazy to spend a fortune on high quality furniture, it pays to go for the medium range furniture if you can afford it. Cheaper quality usually means you will have to replace it sooner with no long term cost savings.

Also, the most successful business is built on repeat business and referrals and rentals are no different. The nicer your home looks, the more likely you are to get returning clients.

Myth: I don't need to use a rental management company

Trying to save money by not using a rental management company could well cost you more money in the long run. Who will keep an eye on the property and let you know if there have been any leaks, breakages or worse robberies?

You also have to consider that if there are any problems with the house you may have to try and

"Community rules are also important - the size of swimming pool and whether a lifeguard is required to be in attendance during opening times - our experience has meant that the opening times are more restricted because of this. Moreover, the Spanish do not want the pool open early or late in the season which also has an impact on us Brits."

www.casahibiscus.com

⊘ Costs to Include

- ❑ Accessories e.g. Mirrors, teaspoons, rugs, pictures etc.
- ❑ Advertising
- ❑ Beddings
- ❑ Community fees
- ❑ Furnishings
- ❑ Furniture
- ❑ Garden furniture
- ❑ Garden maintenance
- ❑ Pool maintenance
- ❑ Property Management
- ❑ Taxes
- ❑ Utility bills
- ❑ White goods

"Furnishing the property was about twice as expensive as was mentioned when we purchased the house."

www.casahibiscus.com

⊕ Use www.kyero.com for free translation of all the core advertising phrases you will need – select all the terms you want to include and click the translate button at the bottom of the page.

coordinate builders, plumbers and other tradesmen to have access to the house. How easy do you think that will be when you are in a different country?

Property Management does not necessarily mean using the services of a large expensive company. "Property Management" means that you have someone, be it a professional company, a friend, cleaner etc, that is willing and able to visit the property on a regular basis, check for any problems, co-ordinate tradesmen and give access to the property for your rental clients.

Myth: I will get enough clients from the English-speaking market

You are missing out on a large share of the rental market if you do not target the Spanish simply because of the language barrier. Use an agency to attract the Spanish clients while you can generate business from English speaking clients with no agency fees.

Myth: I can use it for holidays

The peak holiday seasons are exactly the times when you are most likely to get clients and when you can charge the most for your property rental. If you use it for friends and family or personal use you are unlikely to get much income if any!

Run your buy-to-let as a business

Myth: The letting agent will get me all the bookings I need

Even with the best intention in the world, a letting agent is unlikely to be able to get your property rented the whole year round. Not only will there be thousands of properties available for rent in the area, if you live on a large urbanisation you will also have to compete with possibly hundreds of very similar properties. The only way to maximise your rental income is to run it as a business and that means advertising in as many places as possible.

Find a property management company that speaks English before any problems occur.

www.rentcalendar.com provides a free rental availability calendar in 6 languages.

www.rentalsystems.com is an all in one service for buy-to-let owners allowing you to take credit card bookings, sample rental contracts, advertising on *www.villarenters.com* and much more.

Sample rental contracts in 7 different languages... *www.rentalia.com/owner/legal.cfm*

Do not take rental bookings until you have the keys

Myth: I will make xxx amount from the rental

The clients may pay you xxx amount but you then have to pay the cleaner, the gardener, the repair man, the pool man, the rental management company, replace any broken items in the house, credit card booking charges, etc.

You should estimate that 25% of the rental income will need to go on various costs and charges associated with the rental.

Myth: I will get loads of leads from my website

There is no denying that if you have a dedicated website for your rental property it will help to sell it better as you can include detailed area information, maps, photographs and other helpful information. However, it is pointless having a website if no one is going to see it. There are millions of websites advertising rental properties and publishing your own means nothing unless you can get it to the top of the search engine listings - neither an easy nor cheap undertaking.

Use your website as an added tool to make your property stand out from the rest and provide more than just the basic information you are allowed on rental websites – not as your only advertising option.

When you advertise your property whether on a property portal, in an advertisement or your own website make sure you include as much information as possible. Clients are buying a holiday not a room in a hotel so they will need to know why they should choose your property above all the others.

What You Should Include When Marketing Your Property

What is it close to? Golf, beach, restaurants… Clients need to know they will not be stuck out in the middle of nowhere miles from anything, unless that's what they want.

What facilities does it have? You need to include items such as dishwashers, washing machines, television, radio, games, private or communal swimming pool.

"The firm lost all interest in us after we paid the deposit to them. After that time trying to get any information was like pulling teeth. We had to make several staged payments to the developer as the building continued. We soon discovered that for every payment from UK Pounds to Euros, we had to pay not only the exchange rate, which we expected, but huge amounts were taken by the Spanish Bank too. The 'firm' was not interested. Not their problem, but we could only make the payment through THEIR bank and so we had no alternative. Then, the summer happened. Building ceased for the summer and so our hopes of completing on the house and letting out for that summer were dashed."

www.casajacaranda.com

51

What activities can they do while they are there? Let them know of any water parks, commercial centres, nature parks, water sports etc. in the area. Make sure to include a wide range of topics to ensure you appeal to all age groups and interests.

What makes your property unique? Does it have a roof terrace, large garden, sea views?

FINCAS

Many expats looking to relocate or retire in Spain decide to opt for a *finca* (rural property) as their dream home. The idea of living in the country, getting a bargain and having your large garden to "potter around in" seem like a good idea at the time. Buyers can be seduced by the amount of land they can buy for a low price and if the *finca* needs reforming, the dream of turning it into a country retreat (also known as the poor man's villa.)

The Property Register and Land Register are not necessarily in sync!

However, fincas were traditionally used as buildings to escape the sun or have a rest for farmers tending to their crop or animals. So they are likely to be very basic (unless already renovated) and not very big. Building permissions can be restrictive even if you have a large plot of land so you may not be able to extend the house to a size you want. Make sure you check this before buying the property.

All of the problems associated with modernising a finca are the same as those in the section on renovating property and owners almost always find that they spend far more than originally planned.

In addition to which you will find yourself facing unique "problems" in a finca, for example, you might only have a generator for your electricity and to get connected to the mains you may have to wait several months. When you are connected to the mains the electricity will sometimes fail during heavy rainfall so you will need to ensure you have torches and candles.

✪ Check the details of your plot are the same as those registered at Catastro

🌐 Castastro Offices - where you can find the nearest office to you... *https://ovc.catastro.meh.es/CYCBienInmueble/OVCListaPIC.htm*

🌐 Catastro Virtual Office - where you can view a map of the property if you have the reference number... *https://ovc.catastro.meh.es/CYCBienInmueble/OVCConsultaBI.htm*

✪ Double your original budget when planning finca renovations.

✪ If the finca is close to a town, make sure you check if it is included in any future planning (PGOU).

If the finca does not yet have a telephone installed you may have to wait several months to have any chance of getting a phone line unless it is in an area being heavily developed. It is not unheard of to wait 6 months to a year!

The majority of fincas will have a cesspit rather than mains sewage. This will have to be emptied every so often and if the builders did not put a u-bend in your toilet you may have the delightful smell wafting back into your house.

You are likely to get your water supply from a well rather than mains, which while a free source of water is subject to its own problems. For example, if you have an artesian well with a pump and there is a power cut, you won't have any water – no electricity, no power to the pump - no water. If you have a traditional well – where you can draw the water up with a bucket if need be, this might dry up in the summer and you may have to consider installing an artesian well.

"One summer we were left without water for three days in 40 degree heat. You don't realise how much you take it for granted until you don't have it."

⊛ Get the number of a local handyman who will be able to fix any problems such as the well if you are not able to do it yourself.

It's a fact that you get more "wildlife" in the countryside to contend with than if you were living by the coast e.g. mosquitoes, flies, rats, mice and snakes.

Fail-proofing Your Dreams

THE MOST COMMON REASONS FOR EXPAT FAILURE

Assumptions

This has to be the top reason for failure as it is valid for all aspects of the expat experience. Assuming Spain can't be that different; assuming you can live on less money; assuming you will find work; assuming you can start your own business; assuming you don't need to learn Spanish; assuming everyone will speak at least some English; assuming it won't be that much of a culture shock.

✪ Visualise what it would be like to move to a different area of your country, the changes you would have to make, the things you would miss etc. and multiply it by at least 20 for moving to Spain.

Lack of Financial Planning

Almost everyone spends more than they originally planned for one reason or another. Mixed in with the inability to find well-paid work or unsuccessful business ventures this is undoubtedly one of the top reasons expats return home.

Missing Friends and Family

Many expats find themselves in a catch-22 situation when they move to Spain. While they may love the lifestyle, the country and the culture, they just find it too hard to be so far away from friends and family.

Running Away From Something

Be it emotional problems, boredom or even something as trivial as the bad weather it is important that you move to Spain because you like it and that you do not use it only to run away from something at home.

www.nativespain.com provides a community where expats and locals can share their experiences and make new friends. You can also keep a diary to share with family and loved ones in your old country.

SUCCESSFUL EXPATS

Successful expats are those who...

- Accept that they will need to change and adapt to a new lifestyle and culture

- Appreciate the benefits of living in Spain including a healthier lifestyle, better weather, friendly people, great food

- Make the effort to socialise with their Spanish friends, colleagues and neighbours

- Plan their move carefully, researching where they want to move to before diving head first into a whole new way of life

- Budget realistically so that lack of finances does not ruin their experience

- LEARN SPANISH!

TESTING THE WATER

Many people decide to move to Spain because they have been on holiday and thought, "wouldn't it be great to live here?"

One or two weeks of slapping on the sun cream can be entertaining and a necessary evil for that perfect tan. But if you are serious about moving to Spain (after you have completed all of your research, decided what you can afford and know where you want to live) then your next move should be to take holidays in your chosen area (extended as long as possible) at the most extreme times of the year i.e. mid-summer and mid-winter.

⊗ Consider renting for a month or two before making the decision to sell up back home and move to Spain permanently.

Winter

If the weather is a great motivating factor in you moving to Spain you need to know what it will be like in the coldest, darkest months. You will doubtless have in your mind the typical image of "Sunny Spain". In Costa de la Luz, it can go from -4 in the mornings to 18 degrees in the afternoon. That is a huge 22 degree difference in the South of Spain! And should you choose to live in a mountainous region you will find that the winter is much like the UK with freezing weather and the chance of getting snowed in. Galicia, for example, that beautiful green province is green because it rains a lot!

If you are desperately missing friends and family and happen to arrive in the short period of time when it is raining and gloomy, it can make it extremely hard to stay positive and "Sunny Spain" can seem a long way away.

If you're moving to Spain for the excellent weather then research, research, research. "Sunny Spain" can also include "Rainy Spain" and "Snowy Spain"

Try to move in spring or autumn to avoid extreme temperatures

Check Weather Averages www.*weather.msn.com/m onthly_averages.aspx?&we alocations=wc:POXX0013& setunit=F*

You also need to know what that bustling coastal resort is like in winter when the tourist population has left. If the area you choose to live in caters predominantly for tourists, which means that out of season restaurants and bars will be closed, there will no longer be the same atmosphere that made you fall in love with the place.

"The first house we stayed in was so cold we had to buy thermal sleeping bags and go to bed fully-clothed for about two months."

Summer

Or perhaps you have only visited out of season? Which is precisely why you should go back to the area at the height of the tourist frenzy in August.

The population of some towns can increase three or four times, gorgeous deserted beaches will become a heaving mass of sweaty bodies and parasols, and the invasion of the holiday brigade might make you see the place in a different light.

✪ Visit your target location during both peak and off season so you don't get any nasty surprises.

You should allow yourself time to adjust to the climate so that it does not become a factor that makes you decide to return home. The heat of the full summer in Spain, often reaching well over 40 degrees in some areas, can be unbearable for some.

Food

Have you considered what it will be like to be without your local supermarket favourites? Eating in your local Spanish tapas bar at home or having a week of "foreign food" on your holidays is not the same as living full time in Spain. Why do you think there are so many fish and chip shops or bars offering "roast beef" in the most popular tourist areas? Humans are creatures of habit and tend to want what they are used to.

The sausages are not the same, the tea tastes different, gravy? What's that? Deprivation makes you crave the strangest things. And if you do find some old favourites they are likely to be imported just to cater for the "gringos" and will be much more expensive.

✪ When on holiday only eat local dishes or buy Spanish style food at the supermarkets

✪ Make a list of things you can't live without for visitors to bring over!

Success Stories

RETURN TO ENGLAND?
NOT LIKELY!

I arrived in Spain from England to start a new life with my husband and two small boys. I remember it clearly, 26th March 2003, we left England on a beautiful unseasonably hot and sunny afternoon only to arrive in Huelva (that well known part of Spain) to electric storms, torrential rains and a power black out. I got into bed that night thinking "What have we done?"

Michaela Lloyd

What we had done (which on reflection seems a little impulsive) was to purchase a holiday home in a part of Spain that we had never visited before prior to the inspection visit and subsequently decided 2 years later that it was where we wanted to live and bring up our children!

When we commenced our search for a holiday home in partnership with my brother we were all clear on the requirements. The area should be family orientated, definitely no "beer bellies" or "all day breakfasts". We wanted traditional Spanish pueblos, beautiful beaches, golf and with a drive of no more than 1 hour from the nearest international airport.

We found all of this on the Huelva coast of Costa De La Luz. The majority of properties within the coastal resorts are owned by Spanish and Portuguese city folk and English is not widely spoken. We bought a property on Islantilla golf course and just 10 minutes walk to the beach.

"We began to question our lives in England more than previously and began to realise that we wanted more quality of life."

After spending several holidays in our newly purchased house it soon felt like I was coming home every time we drove over the River Guadiana Bridge towards Ayamonte from Portugal.

We began to question our lives in England more than previously and began to realise that we wanted more quality of life and we wanted out of the rat race (we both worked in the IT Telecoms sector in London.)

We wanted a relaxed open environment for our sons Freddie and Joe to grow up in and to be able to spend more time outdoors (in pleasant weather where we would see the sun on more of a daily basis) and to enjoy a different culture and language.

Peter decided to accept a job offer with the company that had sold us our holiday home and we then commenced the detailed search for schools and a permanent home to live in. We felt that living in a holiday resort is not the same as living in a residential area with all of the infrastructure and facilities that goes with it, plus you have the added benefit that your neighbours don't change every 2 weeks! We were on our way!

Pete left his new job after 2 years to buy into a partnership of a business based in Aljaraque.

Freddie and Joe now attend the local public school; they are both bilingual and speak Castellano Spanish with an Andalucian accent! The majority of

"We wanted a relaxed open environment for our sons to grow up in."

their friends are Spanish with just a handful being of mixed Spanish/British decent.

So, what about me? I discovered isolation and loneliness in the first year having not really considered the impact of Pete being at work all day and me staying at home with the kids. I didn't know anyone at all and there wasn't another English speaking person to communicate with day in day out! Also I underestimated the emotional impact of missing friends and family. I was lucky that I met some very special people after our move to Bellavista and I have been supported through some very challenging times including the very sudden death of my mother last year.

"I underestimated the emotional impact of missing friends and family."

But now, many of my friends that I see on a day to day basis are Spanish, we go to Pilates and dance classes, meet in the park with the kids in the afternoons and I am helping them to learn some English. Being engrossed in the local community and mastering the language completely is

I believe essential to the continuing success of our lives here in Spain.

Have we achieved what we set out to? Yes, I would say that we have. Has it been easy? Definitely not! We have had our ups and downs just like everybody else and at times it has been an up hill struggle. Would I willingly return to England? Not Likely!

YOU'D HAVE TO BE MAD TO WANT TO LEAVE HERE

I came over to Spain in 1992 for one year and now, 15 years later I'm still here. The reason I stayed was quite simple. I fell in love with the place, the lifestyle, the easygoing nature of the people and the weather. I also met a Spanish woman fell in love, got married and had a family. I worked in education, teaching English in schools and academies and really enjoyed what I was doing.

Kieran O'Reilly

AndalusianHouse.com

The first couple of years were difficult trying to get a handle on the language. The accent in Huelva, Costa de la Luz, could be described as a cross between a broad Geordie accent and an east end Cockney accent, however with the help of not only my wife but with the good friends I made, I was soon progressing. I thought to myself that if I can learn Spanish here I will understand it anywhere.

"I thought to myself that if I can learn Spanish here I will understand it anywhere."

After 10 years in the education system and armed with a fairly decent level of Spanish I decided that the time was ripe to branch out and try new things. I got speaking to some Spanish friends who persuaded me to come in with them on a business venture they were setting up. They wanted to start up a real estate business in the area and basically needed a native English speaker who could help target the foreign, particularly British and Irish property buyers. I became a full partner in AndalusianHouse.com and jumped into the world of real estate, at first trying to learn as much as possible.

The first year was a steep learning curve but very enjoyable and we survived. At times it was tough but we persevered and managed to keep the company afloat. On a personal level it was challenging in that I was moving into a new world and getting to grips with language and jargon I wasn't used to and dealing with builders and clients. But I knew that once we got over the initial learning experience it would even out, and it did.

There was more travelling involved and of course longer hours. Running your own business means that you can't really have time off. I learnt to take something positive from every experience and make use of it. I had to make it work because the thought of going back to teaching didn't appeal to me and to be honest I enjoyed the challenge of selling land and property.

"The first year was a steep learning curve but very enjoyable and we survived."

"There is no way I could ever leave and go back to Ireland. The wet and cold would kill me. You'd have to be mad to want to leave here."

The principal reason we are successful is that we are selling products that we totally believe in. My partner and I both came to this area and fell in love with it and settled here so in effect we are walking advertisements. The area sells itself. The weather and the white beaches and of course the food and wine all taken in a relaxed manner all add up to a wonderful way of life. When I am asked by clients who are simultaneously pointing to the blue skies, "How often is the weather like this?" I tell them, "All the time". And it is. Over 3000 hours a year sunshine!

Sometimes the clear blue skies everyday do get me down and I long for the cloudy and soft days of Ireland, but those days are few and far between. The job has made me travel into Portugal a lot more and has opened my eyes to the beauty on my doorstep which I never really looked at before. Here we have two distinct cultures side by side and each is unique. They are both beautiful countries with wonderful people. There is no way I could ever leave and go back to Ireland. The wet and cold would kill me. You'd have to be mad to want to leave here.

ALL WORTHWHILE IN THE END

My move to Spain had all of the ingredients for a smooth transition and a fairy tale story of life in a new country. I was moving to Spain with a job – to open a new office with the company I worked for. We sold our UK house so had money in the bank. My children were 3 and 5 years old – young enough to easily adapt. My husband was as keen to move as I was. And the best bit of all I am bilingual as my parents are Spanish!

Yet despite all of this, the first two years in Spain were a real struggle both emotionally and financially. Everything just seemed to be so difficult. An impatient caffeine junkie from London, I chose to come to one of the most laid-back parts of Spain – and the change of pace of life

Yolanda Solo

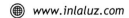 *www.inlaluz.com*

73

was almost unbearable when having to deal with the "administration".

It took at least two years for me to finally relax, when I realised that at least half of the problem was with me. The reason it was so hard was that I had made mistakes financially, failed to plan properly and was still "assuming" things would work in a certain way.

"The first two years in Spain were a real struggle both emotionally and financially."

Despite all of the problems however, I always knew that I did not want to go back to the rat-race lifestyle of London. So now instead of putting the blame on Spain, I look around me while sitting, drinking my coffee in the sunshine (relaxed at a cafe bar instead of gulping it while dodging the thousand of commuters at Liverpool Street station) and remember why I made the move in the first place.

The lifestyle, the people and of course the weather make it all worthwhile in the end.

GOING NATIVE IN MURCIA

"Eh, hombres, enhorabuenas!" Miguel El Gordo shouted at me and my husband Marcus, over the din of that night's "entertainment."

The second night of our *fiesta* was punctuated with the clamour of a heavy rock band. It was two in the morning and they had only just begun - over three hours later than advertised. But that wasn't their fault; the electrical generators in the disused quarry just couldn't cope with the "10,000 watts of sound and 24,000 watts of light!" They had already blown two generators the size of small cars and were now on their third!

Debbie Jenkins

Co-author of
*"A Brit's Scrapbook:
Going Native in Murcia"*
www.nativespain.com

The quarry was heaving. The *sobrasada* and *cerveza* were flowing. Young children were screaming with glee and racing around the legs of tables, adults and the makeshift beer tents. Even the oldest partygoers were raring to go on all night -

dancing, gyrating and generally enjoying the party atmosphere.

"Congratulations for what?" we screamed back in between the chorus and the big guitar solo.

"You're on the fiesta committee for next year!" Miguel grinned and then he winked, coughed, spat and ambled off to tell his good news to our other friends in the village.

"After 18 months living in this totally Spanish village of 101 people, we were now on the inside of the most important part of village life."

So, we'd been accepted. After 18 months living in this totally Spanish village of 101 people, we were now on the inside of the most important part of village life – the *Fiesta Patronale*.

Three years earlier we'd decided to leave the hustle and bustle of the city behind and find a better quality of life where the climate and the people were much warmer.

Before we moved we lived in a 3 storey Victorian terraced house in the UK's second largest city - Birmingham. My husband, Marcus, had a well-paid career with an International consulting company and

I ran my publishing business from offices in the city centre. Our family was in striking distance, we had plenty of friends and what most would consider a good life. But we yearned for something more.

We wanted to swap grey concrete, monotony, anonymity, rain, crime and stress for mountains, oceans, trees, variety, a sense of belonging, sunshine, adventure and relaxation. We got La Murta on the Costa Cálida in Southern Spain. Perfect.

"We avoided the expat and tourist hotspots and looked for places well off the beaten track."

It took us almost two years to find our perfect spot after visiting different parts of the country 8 times! We knew we wanted to be a part of real Spain so we avoided the expat and tourist hotspots and looked for places well off the beaten track. We ended up with a cave house and 20,000 m^2 of land on the Costa Cálida in the Murcia region.

Marcus and I had worked hard to learn Spanish (Marcus more successfully I might add) during our search and so we made friends easily with our neighbour, David, a stocky, handsome and hard-working man in his 80's who fled to France when Franco was in power.

As we bought a cave house it's not the usual renovation project! We've spoken with a number of builders and architects who all have different ideas of what we should do. In the meantime, we decided to build a second property, which is complete, so we now live in this second house while we manage the cave renovation project.

Owning such a remote place does provide its challenges however. We have to have water delivered by lorry where leaky plumbing between the "water cubes" and our house is an expensive, and all too frequent, inconvenience. We had no toilet facilities (as the building work on our drainage system wasn't quite complete) for 3 weeks after we moved in and our electricity relied on 2 small petrol generators and car batteries for over a year. Thankfully, we've now got mains electricity, which was by no means as simple and easy as the estate agent said it would be!

"We had no toilet facilities for 3 weeks after we moved in."

Neighbours take on greater importance out in the countryside of Spain too.

In England you can live in a street of a few hundred people in terraced houses, hear their arguments, love-making, eating and fun – and never really know them. Here, in Spain, you are immediately adopted into the Spanish families, welcomed, fed, educated, entertained and good naturedly interrogated about what you've been up to. In return you provide them with news, stories and an exotic slice of a different world.

Our life is fuller than ever in Spain. We've just hit almond picking season and as we have over 400 trees that need to be picked by hand this is taking up a lot of our free time.

"Our life is fuller than ever in Spain."

Other "chores" include walking our two dogs – Dani and Fuggles – who often run off only to come back tired, smelly but extremely happy hours later. We are in the natural park, so walks up the mountain and around the pine forests and *ramblas* (dried up river beds) are a twice daily event.

When we're not busy looking after the land, fixing leaky plumbing or searching for missing dogs we have plenty of other pursuits too.

Since moving here we've become active and enthusiastic scuba divers and most Sundays we'll be found under the water of the Mediterranean. We're spoilt for choice for dive sites; within an hour we can be at the coast and geared up for a dive.

"When we're not busy looking after the land, fixing leaky plumbing or searching for missing dogs we have plenty of other pursuits too."

On a Sunday morning we'll often head into Murcia city where we consume coffee, tapas and newspapers in the pretty Cathedral square. In the afternoon Marcus does clay pigeon shooting (which is much more accessible and cheaper in Spain than the UK) while I paint – a hobby inspired by the majestic beauty of our surroundings.

I cook and prepare fresh food almost every day, usually fresh local salad and locally butchered meat or fish. We live in an area that is known as the "market garden", so we have an abundance of local produce. The "food miles" have reduced enormously – more like "food feet" now. When we do eat out the price for a 3-course lunch (including wine) during the week is less than 10 Euros and it is excellent quality.

I say on a regular basis that the Spanish "take having fun seriously". They live a full life here. They spend time with friends and families. They make an effort to enjoy themselves on a regular basis and fill their lives with fun. By being selected for the fiesta commission we've effectively been accepted into the most sacred aspect of village life. The fact that we're foreigners – *mad ingleses* – to boot is also testament to the inclusiveness and warmth of our new neighbours and validates our reasons for moving here.

In addition to our home in La Murta we recently bought a large townhouse which we're converting into 2 rental properties – *www.moratallatownhouses.com*

"The 'food miles' have reduced enormously – more like 'food feet' now."

MORATALLA HERE WE COME!

My wife Julie and I swapped our home in Great Yarmouth for a traditional townhouse in Moratalla in December 2007 after an extended, cold, wet and windy viewing trip the previous October.

One of my key criteria for our house in Spain was that it had to be CHEAP! Being further inland, Moratalla house prices are much lower than other, more coastal parts of Murcia and furthermore - locals prefer to live in the modern part of town meaning prices are even lower in the older quarter. So, based on the low house prices I wasn't expecting much but after a short walk around Moratalla (even though it was pouring with rain at the time!) I fell in love with it.

So we now live in a 4 storey townhouse high up in the old quarter of Moratalla near to the main church square. Being a Moorish town this means narrow, winding streets, balconies overflowing with plants and flowers that almost meet and

Joe Gregory

www.bookshaker.com

"One of my key criteria for our house in Spain was that it had to be cheap!"

neighbours attached to our house from above, below, to both sides and even to the rear!

Although we originally bought our house over a year ago, getting all our stuff in order in the UK took longer than we anticipated. Things we've had to do have included renting out our UK house (just in case we decide to come back), making essential job contacts for my wife, rehoming our 2 elderly cats (we couldn't bear to make them fly that far) and my wife learning to drive (which is essential for her job now we're in rural Spain without the luxury of regular buses and trains).

"Getting all our stuff in order in the UK took longer than anticipated."

Also, as there is a lot of renovation going on in Moratalla, builders are in very short supply. Finding people in Spain, who aren't super expensive or too busy to do the work, to renovate our house has been like finding the proverbial needle in a haystack. So, in addition to spending a summer holiday doing essential maintenance work ourselves, we've had to call in the building skills of my father.

On the work front we're in a better position than many as I co-run a small publishing business that can be operated from anywhere with an internet connection. However, my wife has abandoned a stable sales job in the UK for a less than perfect commission-only post with a real estate company in Spain. It's early days so we don't really know if this will work out well but, as Julie's Spanish isn't up to scratch yet, she accepts that job opportunities for a foreigner are more limited.

"My wife has abandoned a stable sales job in the UK for a less than perfect commission -only post in real estate."

We've had plenty of challenges so far too. We decided to get a Spanish mortgage to buy our house but hadn't quite realised that lenders in Spain aren't quite as generous as they are in the UK. This meant we needed a bigger deposit than we first anticipated (paid for with a loan in the UK) and the fees we paid to our mostly useless, and very slow, mortgage broker were bordering on daylight robbery.

In essence, getting a mortgage with a rubbish rate (thanks to us having no credit history in Spain and buying a ruin) took absolutely ages. The mortgage brokers (who got paid far more than they deserved) and solicitor (likewise) had missed some really crucial "errors" in the paperwork which would have been very bad for us had my brother-in-law (who's Spanish is excellent) not read through them too.

We've also had to adjust to a massive slowdown in the pace of life. Having only recently moved from a large city to Great Yarmouth - I had already slowed down a bit but if people in Norfolk tend to be laid back, the people in Moratalla are almost horizontal!

But do I miss hectic, rude, pushy and stressed people all fighting to get ahead? Not really! If I'm really honest I can't say there is much to leave behind in the UK except the nasty weather, bad service, overpriced food and drink and exorbitant heating costs.

The really wonderful thing about Moratalla for me is that you really feel like you're living IN a community. We have a bakery 2 doors to the right

"I can't say there is much to leave behind in the UK except the nasty weather, bad service, overpriced food and drink and exorbitant heating costs."

"Every time I drive up towards Moratalla and see it perched on the side of the mountain with its distinctive castle and church jutting up towards the sky - I have to smile!"

and bars scattered all along the street which leads to a handful of shops a butcher and even a theatre further down the hill. The smell of woodsmoke (from the bakery) mixed with fresh baked bread, coffee from the bars and the pine forest just out of town gives Moratalla a unique, welcoming scent too.

Every time I drive up towards Moratalla and see it perched on the side of the mountain with its distinctive castle and church jutting up towards the sky - I have to smile!

If you like parking space then living in a townhouse here won't be for you though. We have to park 5 minutes walk away from the house and only drive past to drop off shopping and heavy stuff we don't want to lump from the car.

My only real regret is that I wish I'd started learning Spanish sooner and more methodically before I got here. Despite working really hard over the last year my Spanish is still pretty awful.

Planning & Preparation

Now we get to the stage where the real work begins!

Having 1) made the decision you want to move to or invest in Spain and 2) Researched where you want to buy or invest, you must now arm yourself with the tools to make your venture successful.

LANGUAGE

Language is one of the biggest barriers to moving to a new country but a surprising number of people decide to relocate knowing little if any of the language of the country they are moving to. The intention is there and you may open the dictionary once or twice before you leave, but it is easy to get lost in your priorities when you are trying to reorganise your entire life.

"As my parents are Spanish a lot of people assume that I must speak it perfectly. Yes of course I have an advantage, but I was born and raised in England and my parents spoke English at home. What they don't see is when my husband sends me to Leroy Merlin (equivalent to B&Q) to buy a strimmer.
CONTINUES...

...CONTINUED

I had no idea what it was called so the best I could do was say in Spanish 'have you got the thing for the garden that goes brrrrrrrrrrrrr rrrrrrrrrrrrrrrrrrrr' while swinging my arms wildly left to right.

"Did I look ridiculous? Of course I did, but the assistant knew what I meant straight away and we both had a good laugh at my impression of a mad woman with an imaginary machine gun."

It is also easy to assume that most people speak English, especially if you move to an area with a large expat population. However, you are still moving to a foreign country. The Spaniards are not obliged to be able to speak your language, it is up to you to adapt to Spain. There are so many situations where you will need to speak Spanish and where knowing the basic *"si"*, *"gracias"* and *"dos cervezas por favor"* will just not be enough.

Not only will you be in a country with a different language, there are different accents and regional dialects which can seem like a completely different language to a non-Spanish speaker.

Let us take Andalucía as an example. Not only do they sound as if they are talking at 100 miles per hour, they also tend to cut off the end of many words. For example:

"No se ha enterado de nada" becomes *"No sa enterao dna"* mixed with a healthy dose of mumbling

translates into absolute gibberish to the non-Spanish speaker.

The fastest way to learn Spanish is to mix with Spanish people and speak the language EACH and EVERY day.

The less Spanish you know before you arrive in Spain, the longer it will take for you to learn. If you do not have time to take Spanish lessons then there are still a host of other options for you to familiarise yourself with the language:

Accelerate your language learning by mixing with Spanish people.

Word of The day

If you are a daily email user you can get a different Spanish word emailed to you each day. It's quick, free and easy.

Language Audio Files

They can be played in the car, on your MP3 player on the way to work, or at home. What's that I hear you say? You don't have time to listen to Spanish tapes/CDs etc? Have you ever calculated how much time you waste driving, commuting to work, watching mindless TV? There are few people who could not find one hour of the day when they could

Combine learning Spanish with your day to day tasks by having Spanish audio on in the background.

combine learning Spanish with their day to day tasks – even if it means listening to it in the background when you are cleaning, getting dressed or having a bath.

Radio

Tune in to a Spanish radio station and listen to it as often as you can. Although you may find it impossible to understand anything at first, it is an excellent way to get used to listening to every day Spanish (as opposed to learning just a handful of Spanish phrases).

Listen to Spanish radio and let the language filter into your subconscious.

The key is not to try and understand everything, simply to let it filter into your subconscious. You may just be surprised at how much you can piece together after doing this for a relatively short time.

Movies

Rent or buy Spanish films which have English subtitles. The more you repeat this the more you will associate what is being said with the English translation – so make sure you find a movie you enjoy and watch it as often as you can.

Find a Spanish film you enjoy and watch it as often as you can. Turn the English subtitles off after a few times and see how much you can understand.

Memory Joggers

Find the translation for all the items you have in your house and stick post-its with the Spanish word all over the house!

Wordchamp.com

One of the best free resources available for learning a language. Choose a website – any website – and when you hover over the words Wordchamp provides a translation and tells you how to pronounce it. You can create vocabulary lists and flashcards so that you can tailor learning Spanish to a topic that interests you.

A very useful free language learning resource...
www.wordchamp.com

One of the great things about Spain is that there is an almost year-long café culture and the people are very open and friendly. So if you are new it will only take a small effort to get to know people. Whether you become a local at a bar/cafe, or you do the school run, the fact you are a foreigner can work in your favour as it is a topic of conversation.

⊛ Ask Spanish people you meet (even if they have good English) to speak to you as much as possible in Spanish.

⊛ Talking more loudly and more slowly to the locals won't make them understand you any better - LEARN SPANISH!

Develop the art of chit-chatting. Who cares if you have the same conversation 100 times? You are interacting, meeting people, making contacts that might bring you work, finding useful people who could save you hours because they know where to get cheap materials, the best food, etc. The list is endless. As time goes on and you build up your group of friends and associates you can choose to do this less and less.

You might just be amazed at how much you get away without knowing, especially in a country that is so expressive that they often do not need to finish a sentence, using instead a shrug of the shoulders and hands thrown up in the air for example.

FINANCE

Many expats still have the idea that Spain is as cheap as it was 15 years ago. Spain has developed a lot since then with the resulting increase in standard of living and property prices.

Do not assume that you can live for half the money that you currently need and base your first six months budget on what you are currently spending. Remember that there is much more to moving to Spain than just paying your food bills and having a bit of spending money.

Almost anyone who has moved to Spain will tell you that they have spent more than they expected to.

While in general it will be cheaper to live in Spain, the climate and lifestyle will mean that you will spend more time outdoors, in cafes etc. and could therefore spend more money.

It is also very easy to have that "holiday" feeling for quite some time, along with which you spend as if you were on holiday rather than budgeting for your long-term lifestyle.

✩ Always overestimate your costs and underestimate your income when creating a budget

"When you are planning your budget, times your estimated costs by 4 and halve your estimated income. You should then come close to a realistic figure."

✩ When planning your move you should try to have the equivalent of one year's wages from the UK saved if you do not have a job organised

✪ Research Spanish wages by looking at job offers on-line to get a more realistic idea of your earning potential

✪ Your income could be as little as a third of what you are used to at home - particularly if you don't speak Spanish!

🌐 Compare wages in Spain...
www.tusalario.es
...and the UK...
www.paywizard.co.uk

WAGES

It is easy to underestimate the differences between UK and Spanish wages, with the resultant eating away of your savings if you fail to plan properly.

Not only do wages tend to be lower in general, remember that your employer will also be paying a hefty social security premium for you each month, which will lower the wages even further.

There are a range of job search sites where you can research the average wages for your area to give you a better idea of your earning potential.

As a very general rule of thumb you can halve the wages you currently earn.

MORTGAGES

Choose your mortgage carefully. While it may be tempting to think that you can change it when you find a better deal, you should be aware that changing a mortgage will incur not only the administration costs of the lending bank, but also the conveyancing and legal costs including the notary. This could be several thousands of euros. Re-mortgaging is very expensive in Spain.

✪ Do not sell your UK home unless absolutely necessary until you are sure you will stay in Spain. Money invested in a house will be spent far less quickly than cash in the bank.

The cost of arranging a mortgage itself can add up to 2% to the purchase. Another good reason for researching carefully which bank you take out your mortgage with, as the administration fee charged by banks can vary substantially.

You should also consider that although you may have savings to live on when you first arrive in Spain, should you decide to apply for a mortgage or any form of credit facility, you will need a work history to qualify for it. As a minimum, three months payslips will be required and if self-employed one or two years of accounts.

If may not seem important initially, but it is best to get pre-approval for a mortgage based on your UK income before you arrive if possible. Remember it may take up to six months to find a property you want to buy and process the paperwork, by which time your UK earnings may no longer qualify.

⊛ Try and get pre-approval for a mortgage before you arrive.

Before you move or invest in Spain research the Spanish banks that you would consider getting a mortgage with. It is not just the lowest rate that is important – if they oblige you to take out a pension plan, life insurance and who knows what other policies to qualify, the mortgage is not such a good deal anymore.

⊛ Add 10% of the purchase price to property to cover costs.

If you are not a Spanish speaker you also need to find out if they offer bi-lingual online banking and telephone support staff. How exactly will you maintain your account or query any problems if you can't communicate with your bank?

Which is why you should do your research beforehand. There are several international banks offering mortgages in Spain such as Barclays, Halifax, Citibank and a growing number of Spanish banks also offer international versions of their sites.

🌐 Ask a lawyer about property... *www.spainlawyer.com*

PROPERTY

When you are searching for property you should add approximately 10% of the price of the property to cover IVA (VAT), notary fees, lawyer's fees etc.

Example of the costs involved in buying a €100,000 resale property assuming a 70% mortgage:

Property Registry	€274.06	0.27%
Notary	€481.41	0.48%
Administration	€250.00	0.25%
Transfer Tax	€7000	7.00%
Mortgage		
Arrangement Fee	€700	1.00%
Register Search	€12.02	0.02%
Appraisal	€200	0.20%
Stamp Duty	€428.40	0.43%
Property Registry	€256.03	0.26%
Notary	€605.82	0.61%
Administration	€250	0.25%
Total	10,457.74	10.76%

⊛ Mortgage costs are calculated as a percentage of the purchase price. These figures are only an estimate and could well vary depending on the type of property you buy and mortgage you take out.

SCHOOLS

There are many different schools of thought (pardon the pun) on whether you should send your children to a local Spanish school or to an international school.

If you send your children to a local school they will quickly learn the language, make local friends and adapt to the Spanish way of life. However, the initial shock of being thrown into a new school with new friends and having to learn a new language can severely affect many children. And it is also important to consider that if you decide you want to return home after a year, they may have been learning a different curriculum and will most likely speak English with a Spanish accent and so yet again, be the odd ones out.

If you choose to send the children to an international school, it will make the transition easier if you decide to move back home. However, it will also mean that the children are likely

⊛ Talk to locals about schools as they will know which ones are considered the best.

to mix mainly with other English-speaking children.

A bi-lingual school is a good alternative as they are likely to have a mix of Spanish and international children and will continue to learn in English as well as Spanish.

One school model is no better than the others; it very much depends on your plans and which will best suit your children

It's generally considered that the younger the children are the better they will adapt. A key age seems to be about 7 or 8 years old, much older and it begins to get harder as they will have an established group of friends and already be used to a certain school system.

If you are planning to send your children to a fee-paying school, it is easy to forget that you will need to pay the fees for many years to come. While accessible when you first arrive with lots of savings or the proceeds from the sale of your house in your own country it is important to

✪ The younger the children are the better they are likely to adapt to a Spanish school.

"It seemed like a good idea to send the kids to a bi-lingual school when we came over using money from the sale of the house. It seemed really cheap compared to school fees in London. Two years later we are really struggling to pay the fees and might have to take the kids out of a school they love."

remember that you may be looking at over €60,000 to keep two children in school for 10 years – not including extras and inflation.

NABSS - Schools in Spain
www.nabss.org

Research the schools listed on the websites such as the National Association of British Schools in Spain - nabss.org - to estimate the school fees payable in the area of Spain you will be relocating to.

Research schools before the move and include fees in your budget if choosing a private school

Decide on which type of school is most likely to suit your child and research the schools accordingly. If you are going to send your children to a local Spanish school it will make their transition much easier if they start learning Spanish before they arrive.

Remember that applications to schools should be made before April to ensure the best chance of entry into your preferred choice.

You should also apply to schools before April, as this is when applications are received and places allocated. Which is not to say you won't be able to get them a place after this date, just that you will have a better chance of getting them into your first choice of school.

HEALTH

There is a popular misconception that because Spain is part of the European Union that health care will automatically be provided. The old E111 form – which is now extinct - has been replaced by the European Health Insurance Card. The EHIC is valid up to 5 years but only for temporary visits to the European Economic Area. You can apply on-line at: *www.ehic.org.uk*

You should confirm before departure exactly how long your card is valid for and ensure that if you are not working that you have private health insurance.

It only requires one person in the family to pay the social security tariff for the whole family to be covered. However, you must specify who the beneficiaries are as this is not automatic, and each beneficiary will receive their own card, including children.

If you choose to opt for private health care bear in mind that should you choose to set up your own

☆ Make sure you have health cover – whether from your home country, private or from the Spanish state system.

⊕ Information on UK benefits payable when you are abroad... *www.direct.gov.uk/en/Bri tonsLivingAbroad/BeforeY ouGo/DG_4000018*

⊕ European Health Insurance Card - *www.ehic.org.uk*

⊕ Social Security Office *www.seg-social.es*

company, become a freelancer or autonomo, you will be liable for social security payments which could double your health cover costs.

⊕ Documents You May Need

❑ No claims bonus certificate — *If you want cheaper car insurance*

❑ Children's birth certificates — *When registering beneficiaries for social security you need to prove relationship i.e. a full birth certificate which states you are the parent.*

❑ Marriage certificate — *To register spouse as beneficiary for social security*

❑ P60 — *Applying for a mortgage or loan*

❑ 3 months payslips — *Applying for a mortgage or loan*

❑ 3 months bank statements — *Applying for a mortgage or loan*

❑ Children's School Records — *May be requested by private schools to evaluate application*

❑ Vaccination History — *For your doctor in Spain especially with relation to children*

❑ Travel Insurance Documentation — *If you have a long term policy e.g. yearly be sure to check how long your stay can be to be entitled to claim*

❑ Medical Prescriptions — *It will be easier giving your Spanish doctor a prescription with the official names of your medications than trying to explain your history and your systems*

❑ Eye Test Certificate — *This will let your Spanish optician know any problems with your eyes and where your level of vision was at your last check-up - again without having to find the words in Spanish!*

CHANGE OF ADDRESS

If you leave your change of address until you are in Spain it is easy to forget and you may find yourself with debt collection letters for unpaid bills, overpaid child benefit etc.

The easiest way to avoid this is to arrange for a family member or friend to agree to collect your post and forward it to you. After six months, when you have purchased your property or have decided to stay you can then contact the policy companies and give them your Spain address.

Should you choose to use the postal redirection service and miss the renewal date for online applications, you will find that you might have to fly back just to renew and might have missed important post in the process.

While you may be convinced that the move you are making is permanent, nothing is written in stone. You should always allow for the possibility that for a variety of reasons, you may decide to return.

⊘ **Checklist Items**

- ❑ Banks
- ❑ Building Society
- ❑ Shares
- ❑ Child Benefit
- ❑ Council Tax
- ❑ Phone
- ❑ Electricity
- ❑ Gas
- ❑ Television Licence
- ❑ Tax Office
- ❑ Accountant
- ❑ DVLA
- ❑ Doctors
- ❑ Life Assurance
- ❑ House Insurance
- ❑ Building insurance
- ❑ Endowment Policy

If you maintain a UK address and UK bank accounts you are leaving your options open.

FOREIGN EXCHANGE

While you can of course arrange foreign exchange transfers from your overseas accounts to Spain, it is always best to research the foreign exchange brokers before leaving.

✪ Open an account with a foreign exchange broker before you leave.

If possible it is always better to use one recommended by someone you know. However, there are several established and well known agencies listed here.

✪ Sign up for foreign exchange rate updates.

You can also send money from your bank, but it is well known that banks tend to offer lower exchange rates.

It is also well worth signing up to receive email updates on daily exchange rates. If you know you will need to transfer a large sum of money in the next few months talk to your broker about spot exchange rates. You can fix the rate when it is favourable to you and avoid any fluctuations in the forex market,

🌐 **Money Transfers**
www.worldwidecurrencies.com
www.hifx.co.uk
www.travelex.co.uk
www.moneycorp.com
www.currenciesdirect.co.uk

thereby saving yourself hundreds, if not thousands of pounds depending on the amount you transfer.

Conclusion

While this book outlines some of the problems you will encounter when you move to Spain, this is only to ensure you know how avoid them or, at the very least, minimise them. The period of re-adjustment and frustration involved applies not just to Spain but to any major move you will make in your life. Every country has bureaucracy – the real problem being we don't know the rules yet. It seems so much worse because we can't communicate properly and need to learn the new rules in a foreign language.

Intended as an overview of what you need to consider, you should now go and find out the detailed information that is relevant to your particular circumstances and requirements. It would be impossible for one book to cover every eventuality – taxation and documentation alone could be a whole book in themselves!

This book has given you a thorough overview of what to expect – always seek specific advice to match your personal circumstances

More importantly, Spain is a constantly evolving country with changing rules and opportunities. It is essential that you get up-to-date information and advice from a professional.

⊛ With the right attitude, proper planning and realistic expectations – moving to Spain may well be the best thing you have ever done

Use the experience of expats that already live in the area you have chosen, spend time visiting the expat forums which have a wealth of useful information and read the experiences of those who have already moved there. Make a list of the important topics you find and suggestions made, then have any issues confirmed by a professional in the area.

The good news is that with the right attitude, proper planning and realistic expectations, moving to Spain may well be the best thing you have ever done.

The right attitude means that you accept that you will be the "outsider" and have to adapt to the Spanish way of life.

Proper planning means that you need to make sure you are moving for the right reasons, that you can afford to move to or invest in Spain and that you have a plan for survival when you arrive.

Having realistic expectations includes understanding that while you may be poorer financially your quality of life could be much greater, accepting that the first two years may be an uphill struggle but seeing the light at the end of the tunnel and most importantly, having a sense of humour when things do not turn out as planned!

✪ Use the resources, websites and contacts on the following pages to carry on your research!

With these three key ingredients you cannot fail to find your niche in Spain – it may just take a little longer than expected, but then there is always mañana, mañana...

Resources

EMERGENCY NUMBERS

112   Emergency Number for Police,
Fire Brigade & Ambulance

NON-EMERGENCY NUMBERS

091   National Police

092   Local Police

092   Guardia Civil

080   Fire Brigade (Capitals)

061   Ambulance

ACCOUNTANTS

🌐 *www.spainaccountants.com*
English speaking accountants who can process your tax
payments online with communication via email and telephone

CURRENCY EXCHANGE

🌐 *www.currenciesdirect.com*

🌐 *www.escapecurrency.com* - offer an FX Rate Tracker and
foreign currency you can pick up at airports

🌐 *www.hifx.com* - one of the most well-known forex brokers

🌐 *www.moneycorp.com*

- ⊕ *www.travelex.com*
- ⊕ *www.worldwidecurrencies.com* - efficient personal service from this company based in London

DOCUMENTS

- ⊕ *www.ehic.org.uk* - information on the European Health Insurance Card and application form
- ⊕ *www.direct.gov.uk/en/BritonsLivingAbroad/BeforeYouGo/DG_4000018* - report on benefits payable when you are abroad.
- ⊕ *www.dnielectronico.es* - electronic DNI

DIRECTORIES

- ⊕ *www.yellowpagesspain.com* - English directory offering a list of useful services.
- ⊕ *www.paginas-amarillas.es* - Spanish yellow pages with comprehensive listings. Also has street maps, restaurant and hotel directory

DRIVING

- ⊕ *www.dgt.es* - Traffic Office - find your nearest MOT (ITV) centre, information on regulations, forms and more
- ⊕ *www.permisoporpuntos.es* - listing of all of the offences for which you will be deducted points from your licence
- ⊕ *www.spainlawyer.com/guialegal/00_guia.cfm* - legal information on driving your car in Spain, selling a car and importing a car

EMPLOYMENT

⊕ *www.paywizard.co.uk* - compare wages in UK

⊕ *www.tusalario.es – compare wages in Spain*

⊕ *www.ec.europa.eu/eures/home.jsp?lang=en* - EURES - European Job Mobility Portal with job offers in 31 countries and useful information on working in Europe

Online Job Portals

⊕ *www.ambientjobs.com*
⊕ *www.empleo.net*
⊕ *www.exposure-eu.com*
⊕ *www.globalrecruiter*
⊕ *www.faster.es*
⊕ *www.infoempleo.com*
⊕ *www.infojobs.net*
⊕ *www.jobsabroad.com*
⊕ *www.jobtoasterspain.com*
⊕ *www.laborman.es*
⊕ *www.miltrabajos.com*
⊕ *www.monster.es*
⊕ *www.oficinaempleo.com*
⊕ *www.paginas-amarillas.es*
⊕ *www.recruitspain.com*
⊕ *www.secretariaplus.com*
⊕ *www.talentsearchpeople.com*
⊕ *www.thinkspain.com*
⊕ *www.trabajar.com*
⊕ *www.trabajos.com*
⊕ *www.wemploy.com*

ETTs (Temp agencies)

- www.adecco.es
- www.empresasiman.com
- www.iman.com
- www.flexiplan.es
- www.manpower.es
- www.randstad.es
- www.select.es
- www.tutor-rrhh.com

EXPAT RESOURCES

- www.nativespain.com
- www.britishclubworldwide.com
- www.britishexpat.com
- www.costapages.com
- www.easyexpat.com
- www.escapeartist.com
- www.expatriates.com
- www.expat-blog.com
- www.expatnetwork.com
- www.expats-abroad.com
- www.expatwomen.com
- www.expatica.com
- www.expats.org.uk
- www.expatsradio.com
- www.euroresidentes.com
- www.justlanded.com
- www.retiretothesun.com
- www.spainexpat.com

HEALTH

⊕ *www.seg-social.es* - Social Security

HOLIDAYS

⊕ *info.mtas.es/infpuntual/Fiestas2007/calendariolab_02.htm*
Holiday calendar classified by region from the Ministry of Work and Social Affairs.

INTERNET PROVIDERS

⊕ *www.jazztell.com*
⊕ *www.orange.es*
⊕ *www.telefonica.com*
⊕ *www.telefonicainenglish.com*
⊕ *www.ya.com*

GOVERNMENT

⊕ *www.seg-social.es* - Seguridad Social
⊕ *www.extranjeros.mtas.es* - Immigration and Emigration
⊕ *www.aeat.es* - Tax Office
⊕ *www.dgt.es* - Vehicle Licensing
⊕ *www.mec.es* - Ministry of Science and Education
⊕ *www.mtas.es* - Ministry of Work and Social Affairs
⊕ *www.mir.es* - Ministry of the Interior
⊕ *www.meh.es* - Treasury
⊕ *www.map.es* - Ministry for Public Administration
⊕ *www.dnielectronico.es* - Electronic DNI
⊕ *www.fomento.es* - Ministry of Public Works
⊕ *www.mae.es* - Ministry of Foreign Affairs
⊕ *www.mviv.es* - Housing Ministry
⊕ *www.gksoft.com/govt/en/es.html* - Regional Government Bodies

LANGUAGE

- *www.wordchamp.com* - hover over any word on a page and it will show you the translation of the word, an audio clip of how to pronounce it and allows you to create your own vocabulary lists

- www.bbc.co.uk/languages/spanish/lj/index.shtml - quick course from the BBC on basic Spanish

- *www.rocketspanisheasyway.info* - for those who want a quick fix to learn Spanish this course claims you only need to know 138 words to learn Spanish. They let you try it for free with free lessons via email, flashcards and audio lessons.

- *www.how-to-speak.com* - an original format to learn Spanish that teaches you shortcuts to remember verbs in Spanish such as the fact that nearly all English words that end in ATE can be made into Spanish by changing ATE to AR. Offer 4 free lessons.

- *www.learnspanishfaster.com/parentsdown.htm* - Help Your Child Get An Edge in Spanish - a different way to help your kids learn Spanish with the use of cartoons, crossword puzzles, word searches etc. in comic format. They offer free sample pages to test it out on your kids first.

- *www.pdictionary.com* - lots of practice using online flashcard, picture dictionary and fill in the blanks exercises

- *www.spanishspanish.com* - comprehensive site offering printouts of flash cards, verb tenses, useful vocab etc.

- *www.literacycenter.net* - great interactive site for learning the basics and listening to correct pronunciation

- *www.vocabulix.com* - very useful for learning vocabulary with the option to listen to the pronunciation of each word and then test yourself on what you have learnt. Also offers training on verbs and conjugations.

- www.spanishdict.com - Simple to use online dictionary for finding the Spanish translation for words
- www.bbc.co.uk - useful for basic holiday Spanish with downloadable MP3s and printable vocabulary lists. Also has lots of links to Spanish slang, business Spanish and interactive learning activities.

ONLINE TRANSLATORS

- www.reverso.net - easy to use online translator
- www.elmundo.es - very simple to use translator for paragraphs or web pages
- www.worldlingo.com - good translation for a machine!
- www.babelfish.altavista.com - not the most accurate of translators but has the advantage you can use it for visitors to translate your website if you also need to attract Spanish clients and can't afford to have it translated.

LAWYERS

- www.iabogado.com
- www.spainlawyer.com - Comprehensive legal information in English. You can also get email and telephone consultations for a one-off fixed fee
- www.strongabogados.com
- www.daniel-cano.co.uk - English speaking lawyers with offices throughout Spain
- www.notariado.org - Find a notary and other information on the role of notaries in legal procedures

MAPS

- ⊕ www.map24.com
- ⊕ www.maporama.com
- ⊕ www.multimap.com
- ⊕ maps.google.com

MOBILE PHONES

- ⊕ www.happymovil.es
- ⊕ www.orange.es
- ⊕ www.vodafone.es
- ⊕ www.movistar.es
- ⊕ www.yoigo.com

MORTGAGES

- ⊕ www.bestmortgage.es - includes a breakdown of the costs involved in buying a property and a glossary of terms used in the buying process

- ⊕ www.casahipoteca.com

- ⊕ www.interest.com - 12 different calculators so that you can compare mortgages, find out the real APR, compare 15 yrs vs 30 etc.

- ⊕ www.europamortgages.com - Costa del Sol based mortgage broker offering a wide range of mortgages without charging an arrangement fee

- ⊕ www.spanishmortgagecompany.com

- ⊕ www.tiendahipoteca.es

CAJAS DE AHORROS (BUILDING SOCIETIES)

- ⊕ *www.caixamanlleu.com* - Caixa de Catalunyaaixa de Manille
- ⊕ *www.colonya.es* - Caixa de Pollença
- ⊕ *www.caixasabadell.com* - Caixa de Sabadell
- ⊕ *www.caixapenedes.com* - Caixa d'Estalvis del Penedès
- ⊕ www.caixaontinyent.es - Caixa d'Estalvis d'Ontinyent
- ⊕ *www.caixaterrassa.com* - Caixa de Terrassa
- ⊕ *www.caixagalicia.es* - Caixa Galicia
- ⊕ *www.caixalaietana.es* - Caixa Laietana
- ⊕ *www.caixamanresa.es* - Caixa Manresa
- ⊕ *www.caixatarragona.es* - Caixa Tarragona
- ⊕ *www.cajacantabria.com* - Caja Cantabria
- ⊕ *www.ccm.es* - Caja de Ahorros Castilla La Mancha
- ⊕ *www.kutxa.es* - Caja de ahorros y San Sebastián (Kutxa)
- ⊕ *www.cai.es* - Caja de Ahorros de la Inmaculada de Aragon
- ⊕ *www.cam.es* - Caja de Ahorros del Mediterráneo
- ⊕ *www.cajaduero.es* - Caja de Ahorros de Salamanca (Caja Duero)
- ⊕ *www.elmonte.es* - Caja de Ahorros El Monte
- ⊕ *www.arquia.es* - Caja de Arquitectos
- ⊕ *www.cajadeavila.es* - Caja de Avila
- ⊕ *www.cajarural.es* – Caja Rural
- ⊕ *www.cajacampo.es* - Caja Campo
- ⊕ *www.crcs.es* - Caja Rural Castellón
- ⊕ *www.cajamar.es* - Caja Rural de Almería
- ⊕ *www.cajarural.com* - Caja Rural de Aragón
- ⊕ *www.e-ruralgranada.com* - Caja Rural de Granada
- ⊕ *www.crv.es* - Caja Rural Valencia
- ⊕ *www.ruralvia.com* - Caja Rural Jaén
- ⊕ *www.cajacampo.es* - Caja Campo
- ⊕ *www.cajadeburgos.es* - Caja de Burgos
- ⊕ *www.lacajadecanarias.es* - Caja de Canarias
- ⊕ *www.cajaextremadura.es* - Caja de Extremadura
- ⊕ *www.cajaguadalajara.es* - Caja de Guadalajara
- ⊕ *www.cajacirculo.com* - Caja del Círculo de Burgos

- www.cajacanarias.es - Caja General de Ahorros de Canarias
- www.cajalaboral.com - Caja Laboral
- www.cajamadrid.es - Caja Madrid
- www.cajamurcia.es - Caja Murcia
- www.cajaen.es - Caja Provincial de Ahorros de Jaén
- www.cajarioja.es - Caja Rioja
- www.cajasanfernando.es - Caja San Fernando
- www.cajastur.es - CajAstur
- www.cajasur.com - Cajasur
- www.cajavital.es - Caja Vital Kutxa
- www.ibercaja.es - Ibercaja
- www.lacaixa.es - La Caixa Caja de Ahorros Pensiones Barcelona
- www.sanostra.es - Sa Nostra (Caixa de Balears)
- www.unicaja.es - Unicaja

BANKS

- www.activobank.com - ActivoBank
- www.bancamarch.es - Banca March
- www.batlantico.es - Banco Atlántico S.A.
- www.bbva.es - Banco Bilbao Vizcaya (BBVA)
- www.bde.es - Banco de España (BDE)
- www.bancsabadell.com - Banco de Sabadell
- www.bancovitoria.es - Banco de Vitoria S.A.
- www.bancoesfinge.es - Banco Esfinge S.A.
- www.banesto.es - Banco Español de Crédito S.A. (Banesto)
- www.bancoetcheverria.es - Banco Etcheverria
- www.bancofar.es - Bancofar S.A.
- www.bancogallego.es - Banco Gallego
- www.bancogui.es - Banco Guipuzcoano
- www.halifax.es - Banco Halifax Hispania S.A.
- www.bancoinversion.es - Banco Inversión
- www.bancopastor.es - Banco Pastor S.A.
- www.bch.es - Banco Santander Central Hispano
- www.bancourquijo.es - Banco Urquijo

- www.bancozaragozano.es - Banco Zaragozano
- www.ebankinter.com - Bankinter S.A.
- www.bankpyme.es - Bankpyme
- www.barclays.es - Barclays Bank S.A.
- www.bbk.es - Bilbao Bizkaia Kutxa (BBK)
- www.bsnbanif.es - BSN Banif S.A.
- www.citibank.com - Citibank
- www.commerzbank.de - Commerzbank
- www.deutsche-bank.es - Deutsche Bank
- www.fibanc.es - FIBANC Banco de Finanzas e Inversiones S.A.
- www.bancopopular.es - Grupo Banco Popular
- www.hsbc.es - HSBC Bank plc
- www.iberagentes.es - Iberagentes Popular Banca Privada
- www.ingdirect.es - ING Direct
- www.lloysbank.es - Lloyds TSB Bank plc
- www.solbank.com - Solbank
- www.uno-e.com - UNO-E Bank S.A.

NEWS

- www.c-euro.org - useful fact sheets
- www.theoraclecostadelaluz.com
- www.surinenglish.com
- www.thinkspain.com/today
- www.thetenerifesun.com
- www.theresident.eu
- www.theolivepress.es
- www.majorcadailybulletin.es
- www.livingtenerife.com
- www.andalucia.com/magazine
- www.costablanca-news.com
- www.costatropicalnews.com
- www.theentertaineronline.com
- www.essentialmagazine.com
- www.euroweeklynews.com

- www.fuertenews.com
- www.ibiza-magazine.com
- www.in-madrid.com
- www.ic-web.com
- www.yourlocalnewspaper.info
- www.costalevantenews.es
- www.cbnalmeria.com
- www.costadelsolnews.es

PAYMENTS

- www.eurogiro.com - low cost international transfers offered by post offices and some banks. If you click on Members & Partners at the EuroGiro website you can find which banks offer it in your country.

- www.paypal.com - useful for transferring smaller amounts

- www.sun-pay.com - allows you to hold multiple currency accounts and transfer direct to bank accounts for a fixed fee.

- www.co-operativebank.co.uk – low fee transfers for transferring money for less urgent transactions as it takes up to a week – but the fee is only about £8 instead of a percentage of the amount transferred.

- www.westernunion.com - for same day money transfers when you need to send or receive funds asap although with a high transaction fee

PROPERTY

- www.rentalsystems.com - all in one service for buy-to-let owners allowing you to take credit card bookings, sample rental contracts, advertising on Villarenters.com and much more.

- www.escapelet.com - list your rental property for free

- ⊕ www.diysnagreport.com - do your own snagging on a new property instead of waiting for the developers

- ⊕ www.realdata.com/product/16179.shtml - free software that lets you calculate rates or return, refinancing, loan to value ratio, amortization schedule, loan comparison, break even ratio and more.

- ⊕ www.inspectahomespain.com - provide examples of common snagging problems and snagging Inspection services throughout Spain.

- ⊕ www.kyero.com - offers free translation of all the core advertising phrases you will need

- ⊕ www.tinsa.es/tinsa/productos.php?idp=16 - order a valuation of your property from this Real Estate Valuation Company

- ⊕ www.catastro.meh.es/web_ingles/default.htm - Land Registry Office

- ⊕ https://ovc.catastro.meh.es/CYCBienInmueble/OVCConsulta BI.htm - view a map of the property if you have the reference number

- ⊕ www.registradores.org - Property Registry

- ⊕ https://www.registradores.org:444/propiedad/propiedad.jsp - you can request a copy of a nota simple online

- ⊕ www.rentalia.com/owner/legal.cfm - sample rental contracts in 7 different languages

RADIO

- ⊕ www.global.fm - Global Radio FM 96.5
- ⊕ www.spectrumfm.net - Spectrum FM 105.5

Premier Network Radio FM 96.8 107.0 104.9

Coastline Radio FM 97.7

Central FM 98.6 & 103.8

Glossary

CONDITION	CALIDAD
good condition	buen estado
immaculate condition	estado impecable
well presented	bien presentado
tastefully decorated	decorado con buen gusto
refurbished	restaurado
renovated	renovado
newly built	construccion reciente
renovation needed	para reformar
built to high standards	construcción a alto nivel
spacious accommodation	amplio alojamiento
stylish accommodation	alojamiento con estilo
charming property	propiedad encantadora
full of character	con muchos complementos
many special features	muchas caracteristicas
quality residence	residencia de calidad

LOCATION	UBICACIÓN
access to beach	acceso a playa
central	centrico
near transport	junto a transportes
near beach	cerca de la playa
outskirts of town	extraradio
close to town	junto a ciudad
quiet location	zona tranquila
new development	nuevo
close to the sea	junto al mar
close to shops	junto a tiendas
close to port	junto a puerto
close to golf	junto a golf
sought after area	zona de mucha demanda
exclusive development	construcción en exclusiva
first line beach	primera linea de playa
commercial area	zona comercial
frontline golf	primera linea golf

prestigious area	zona de prestigio
popular urbanisation	urbanización popular
close to all amenities	zona de ocio

ROOMS	**HABITACIONES**
attic room	atico
large attic space	gran atico
breakfast room	sala de desayuno
dining area	comedor
dining room with fireplace	comedor con chimenea
separate dining room	comedor independiente
lounge dining area	zona con salón comedor
reception with fireplace	recepcion con chimenea
office	oficina
separate office	oficina independiente
study	estudio
utility room	trascocina
large store room	gran almacen
various store rooms	varios almacenes
dressing room	vestidor
guest cloakroom	aseo de invitados
interior courtyard	patio interior
various interior patios	varios patios interiores

HEATING	**CALEFACCIÓN**
air conditioning	aire acondicionado
pre-installed air-conditioning	preinstalacion de aire acondicionado
heating	calefaccion
central heating	calefaccion central
electric central heating	calefaccion central electrica
oil central heating	calefaccion central de gasoil
gas central heating	calefaccion central por gas
pre-installed heating	preinstalacion de calefaccion
underfloor heating	suelo radiante
underfloor heating throughout	suelo irradiante completo
rooms individually heated	habitaciones con calefacción propia

fireplace	chimenea
open fireplace	chimenea abierta
KITCHEN	**COCINA**
fitted kitchen	cocina amueblada
kitchen diner	cocina comedor
kitchenette	cocina americana
kitchen semi-furnished	cocina semi-amueblada
luxury kitchen	cocina de lujo
BATHROOM	**BAÑO**
en suite	en suite
en suite bathroom	baño en habitación
en suite shower room	ducha en suite
newly fitted bathroom	baños nuevos
shower room	ducha independiente
BUILDINGS	**EDIFICIOS**
guest apartment	apartamento de invitados
guest bungalow	bungalow de invitados
guest house	casa de invitados
independent apartment	apartamento independiente
independent studio	estudio independiente
possibility to build	posibilidad de construir
permission to build	permiso para construir
possibility of extension	posibilidad de ampliacion
with project to construct	con proyecto de construccion
OUTSIDE	**PARTE EXTERIOR**
terrace	terraza
various terraces	varias terrazas
covered terrace	terraza cubierta
sunny terraces	terrazas con sol
roof terrace	azotea
glazed terrace	terraza acristalada
courtyard	patio
patio	patio
barbecue	barbacoa
tennis court	pista de tenis
fruit trees	arboles frutales

vineyard	viñedos
GARDEN	**JARDIN**
automatic irrigation system	sistema automatico de riego
beautiful garden	bello jardín
community garden	jardin comunitario
easily maintained gardens	jardin de fácil mantenimiento
garden	jardín
landscaped gardens	ajardinado
large garden	gran jardín
mature garden	jardín frondoso
picturesque garden	jardín pintoresco
subtropical gardens	jardines subtropicales
PARKING	**APARCAMIENTO**
garage	garaje
carport	muelle
parking	parking
driveway	camino de acceso
underground parking	parking subterraneo
off road parking	parking exterior
double garage	doble garaje
space for garage	espacio para garaje
SWIMMING POOL	**PISCINA**
Swimming pool	piscina
Private pool	piscina privada
Room for pool	espacio para piscina
Childrens pool	piscina para niños
Covered pool	piscina cubierta
Communal pool	piscina comunitaria
Heated pool	piscina climatizada
Outdoor heated pool	piscina climatizada exterior
SECURITY	**SEGURIDAD**
alarm system	sistema de alarma
24 hour reception	recepcion 24 horas
24h security system	sistema de seguridad 24h
automatic entrance	entrada automatica
cctv	circuito cerrado tv

video entry system	sistema de entrada por video
security system	sistema de seguridad
electronic entry system	sistema de entrada electronico
security guard	guarda de seguridad
electric blinds	persianas electricas
fire detector	detector de incendios
pre-installed alarm	preinstalacion de alarma
gated complex	recinto cerrado
UTILITIES	**SERVICIOS**
bottled gas	gas butano
city gas	gas ciudad
electricity	electricidad
solar power	energia solar
water	agua
water deposit	deposito de agua
well	pozo
telephone	telefono

Make your own custom list of property terms at www.kyero.com

Templates & Checklists

RELOCATION BUDGET

It is not just the costs you will incur in Spain you have to consider when you move, but also the liabilities you are leaving behind.

At Home...	ESTIMATED COST	ACTUAL COST
Mortgages, utilities, taxes, and maintenance		
Savings, insurance and life assurance plans, payments		
Removals		

In Spain...		
20% -30% deposit for the purchase of a property		
Rental accommodation while looking for a property		
Mortgage payments		
Purchase of a new car (or two) if you are not bringing one with you		
School fees		
Renovation budget		
Furniture and fittings		
A monthly "wage" until you can find work		
Mobile phone bills		
Social security/private health cover costs		
Company set up costs if you plan to start your own business		
Taxes – on property, rental income, cars...		

CHANGE OF ADDRESS CHECKLIST

Type	Name	Date Told	Address Given
Bank		❏	
Savings Accounts		❏	
Doctor		❏	
Electric		❏	
Gas		❏	
ISA		❏	
Pension		❏	
Stocks		❏	
Water		❏	
Child Benefit		❏	
Telephone		❏	
Will		❏	
Accountant		❏	
Credit Cards		❏	
Store Cards		❏	
Council Tax		❏	
Health Insurance		❏	
Stocks & Shares		❏	

RENOVATION BUDGET

Expensive Items Not Including Furnishings	ESTIMATED COST	ACTUAL COST
❏ Bathroom		
❏ Doors		
❏ Flooring		
❏ Kitchen		
❏ Landscaping		
❏ Planning permission		
❏ Re-wiring of electrics		
❏ Roof		
❏ Swimming Pool		
❏ Terrace		
❏ Tiling		
❏ Well		
❏ Windows		

PROPERTY BUDGET

LOUNGE	ESTIMATED COST	ACTUAL COST
❏ Bookcases		
❏ Chairs		
❏ Chests		
❏ Clocks		
❏ Compact Disc Players		
❏ Curtains, Blinds		
❏ Desk and Accessories		
❏ DVD Players		
❏ Fireplace Accessories		
❏ Lamps		
❏ Mirrors		
❏ Pictures, Decorations		
❏ Rugs, Carpets		
❏ Shelves		
❏ Sofas		
❏ Stereos		
❏ Table Accessories		
❏ Tables		
❏ Television Sets		
❏ Throws		
❏ Media Storage Cabinet		
❏ Radios		
❏ Telephone		

Remember to use one for EACH bedroom you have

BEDROOM	ESTIMATED COST	ACTUAL COST
☐ Bedside table		
☐ Dressers		
☐ Lamps		
☐ Tables		
☐ Chairs		
☐ Desk and Accessories		
☐ Mirrors		
☐ Curtains, Blinds		
☐ Rugs, Carpets		
☐ Blankets, Quilts		
☐ Linens		
☐ Pictures, Decorations		

BATHROOM	ESTIMATED COST	ACTUAL COST
☐ Bath Mat		
☐ Linens		
☐ Bath Sets		
☐ Clothes Hamper		
☐ Curtains, Blinds		
☐ Mirrors		

KITCHEN	ESTIMATED COST	ACTUAL COST
❏ Stove and Range Hood		
❏ Microwave Oven		
❏ Refrigerator		
❏ Freezer		
❏ Dishwasher		
❏ Table and Chairs		
❏ Electrical Appliances		
❏ Pots and Pans		
❏ Silverware		
❏ Kitchen Utensils		
❏ Dishes		
❏ Glasses		
❏ Brooms, Mops		
❏ Cleaning Materials		
❏ Stools		
❏ Clocks		

About Yolanda Solo

I was born in Worthing, West Sussex to Spanish parents from Galicia. I studied French and Spanish at University of North London, which included a year abroad studying in Montpellier, France and Valladolid, Spain.

I then worked in the City of London for several years as a secretary and administrator. I studied Naturopathy part-time for 4 years, but two children and realising it wouldn't pay the bills caused me to give it up, although I must admit it is my real passion.

I'm married to Abelardo Solo of Filipino origin, he moved to London when he was 10. We have two kids, Brandon who's seven and Kira who's five. They have absolutely thrived since we moved here.

I lived in East Ham before moving to Spain. I realised it was time for a change when I came home to find a bullet hole in our fence where there had been a shoot-out with the police and someone was stabbed in the high street in broad daylight over some silly childhood feud.

Strangely around the same time a clairvoyant told me I would move to Spain in 2-3 years time, which I thought was completely ridiculous, as I hadn't even considered it. I went home and told my husband saying "You'll never believe what she said", and his reply was: "Let's go!"

Mr "been-in-the-same-job-for-17-years-since-leaving-school" didn't really like change, as you can imagine, and he was keen! So that started me thinking it was a possibility.

So I found job with a company selling off-plan property in Spain, the advert said: "You could be living and working in Spain within a year". So I took the job, as I didn't plan to come here without work!

I worked with them for a year and came over to open an office for them in Huelva. A year later, I was still sitting in the equivalent of a shed; just a room with a garage door and one table and one chair. So I decided enough was enough. I tinkered around with property management and did some freelance web design and translation for foreigners in the area. A year later it wasn't paying the bills so I went to work for another real estate company.

We live in a finca in Gibraleon, Huelva. We had the usual expat dream: "Oh wouldn't it be nice to have somewhere with a bit of land and a house that we could renovate?" Seemed like a good idea at the time but of course we completely underestimated how much work 10,000m^2 of land would be and as for the renovation, well, money pit comes to mind.

I found the first six months in Spain really hard, the next six months infuriating, the second year frustrating, and in this third year I have finally settled down. And *I* have the advantage that I can speak Spanish!

This book started with an article I wrote regarding the problem I had with social security and nearly getting my car seized. As I was so furious I just kept on adding little bits to the article until suddenly it turned into a book.

If I am not working or spending quality time with the children I am on the computer doing freelance web design or virtual assistant work, or just surfing, I do love the Internet.

"One of the best books there is for expatriates who want a career adventure. This book is packed with examples, tips and, of course, lots of inspiration. Don't forget to pack it before you set off on your new life."

Robin Pascoe, www.expatexpert.com

EXPAT

ENTREPRENEUR

How To Create and Maintain Your Own Portable Career Anywhere In The World

JO PARFITT

www.bookshaker.com

"Alex Pintea is to be congratulated for a job well done. If you are thinking of buying a property in Romania, you should buy this book."
JOHN HOWELL, SENIOR PARTNER, THE INTERNATIONAL LAW PARTNERSHIP LLP

An Insider's Guide

Buying Property in
ROMANIA

The Essential Guide for Investors and Property Developers

Alex I. Pintea

NativePortugal.com

Buying Property in
Portugal

Gabrielle Collison

Insider tips on buying, selling and renting | 2007

A BRIT'S SCRAPBOOK

GOING NATIVE IN MURCIA

SECOND EDITION

The Essential Guide for Visitors, Expats & Homebuyers

MARCUS JENKINS
DEBBIE JENKINS

FREE FLIGHTS TO BE WON

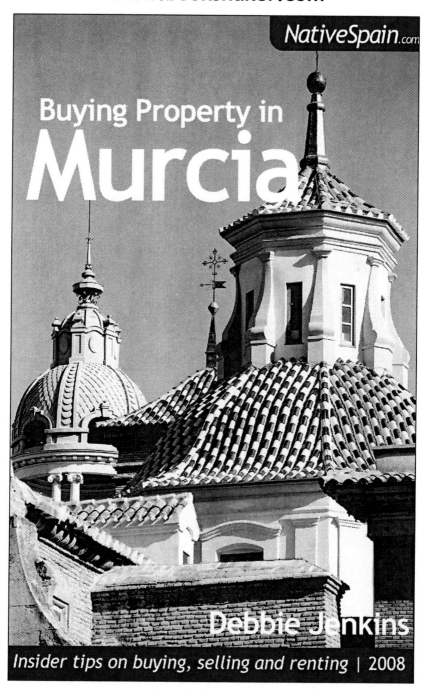

NativeSpain.com

Buying Property in
Murcia

Debbie Jenkins

Insider tips on buying, selling and renting | 2008

Lightning Source UK Ltd.
Milton Keynes UK

177258UK00009B/101/A